About the Author

Paul Clutterbuck was born in England shortly after the Second World War. Throughout his childhood, he suffered the dramatic effects of mercury poisoning from teething powders. Despite this, as a teenager, he played football for Portsmouth F. C. Juniors and England Schoolboys. This was also a time when family traumas dominated. His constant ill-health led to the removal of a lung. At age nineteen, he joined a global computer company.

During the last five decades, Paul has travelled five continents and visited more than forty countries. He has developed an enthusiasm for understanding people and cultures. Living in Amsterdam, Wilmington Delaware and Miami has enriched his life and brought him treasured friendships.

Today he lives in Hampshire with his wife Angela and near their daughters, grandchildren and great-grandchildren. His brother, Peter, is a renowned and talented artistic blacksmith.

To Angela and Willie

Making a Friend Smile

I hope you find
Something in here to
Smile about !

Paul

15th November 2020

Paul Clutterbuck

Making a Friend Smile

Olympia Publishers
London

www.olympiapublishers.com
OLYMPIA PAPERBACK EDITION

A CIP catalogue record for this title is
available from the British Library.

ISBN: 978-1-78830-770-3

This is a work of creative nonfiction. The events are portrayed to the best
of the author's memory. While all the stories in this book are true, some
names and identifying details have been changed to protect the privacy of
the people involved.

First Published in 2020

Olympia Publishers
Tallis House
2 Tallis Street
London
EC4Y 0AB

Printed in Great Britain

Dedication

To Carla, Brendan's wife, who supported him during the
good times and all the really tough moments.

Acknowledgements

To Angela for her support in all things.

One of the most beautiful qualities of true friendship is to
understand and to be understood

Roman Philosopher, Lucius Annaeus Seneca

CONTENTS

Background to The Stories

My friend Brendan was dying of an aggressive, inoperable, brain tumour. In the mid-1970s, against advice and more obvious candidates, he gave me a gift. A wonderful job opportunity which had the greatest positive impact on my working life and consequently that of my family. He gave me a sliding doors moment.[1] The opportunity was a catapult.

In 1979, we lost contact until the summer of 2000. Our families had been friends during the seventies and we easily renewed our friendship. When we learned of his illness, my wife, Angie and I went to visit him and Carla, his wife, in November 2013 — in Minneapolis, Minnesota. He had a few months to live.

Brendan suggested we went for a walk in the woods, just the two of us. I realised he wanted to just walk and see where the talk would take us. I had prepared what I had wanted to say to him a long time beforehand. I told him I wanted to give him a gift.

The two things he had really liked latterly in life were wine and golf. But these weren't possible in his current circumstances. I wanted to write him a letter, once a week, which would be a story of a circumstance in which I found

---

[1] A 'sliding doors' moment is that significant moment in your life where, if you choose to go through a door that slides open for you, your life will take you down a totally different path than choosing not to go through.

myself. I wanted to try and make him smile in the grimmest of personal situations. He liked the idea and he chose the first letter from a list of twenty story headlines I showed him. He then chose the order in which I would write the rest without him knowing what the story was actually about.

This book is my gift to him. He died before I could finish the list, but I continued to write to him. I felt the gift had to be finished. The last time we spoke, he suggested I publish the stories. This book contains the letters I wrote to him before and after he passed.

Foreword

We all meet people in our lives. But rarely comes along someone who actually moves you. Paul Clutterbuck, our author, is one such person. Paul has spirit, a love of adventure and the exotic. But more than all of that, Paul actually cares about people, cultures and getting to know them. On the pages of this book that follow, you will get to know Paul and get to touch that spirit.

Brendan Hegarty is the dying man Paul speaks of. Paul's letters to Brendan not only made him smile, they made him LAUGH. Not an easy task when the reader is dying. Here's to you, Paul! Thank you for making our lives better,

    Carla Hegarty
    Widow

About Brendan Hegarty

Brendan was born in London, the son of Irish immigrants. Education took Brendan away from poverty. He earned a PhD in physics and later, he was awarded an honorary doctorate from the University of Ulster. Brendan progressed rapidly after joining a global computer company, distinguishing himself in positions both in the UK and the Netherlands. He was then assigned to a senior position in San Jose, California where he became a prominent member of the Irish community.

After transferring to another well-known Silicon Valley computer company, Brendan famously met John Hume [2] (Member of Parliament in Northern Ireland and Member of the European Parliament). Mr. Hume came to the US looking for investment for his Derry community. The best example of the impact Brendan made is embedded in the quote from the BBC article on its' website, dated 16th May 2013, on the 20th anniversary of the opening of the Seagate Technology facility in Derry, Northern Ireland.

"It all started out as a friendly chat over a pint and ended with hundreds of millions of pounds cash injection for Northern Ireland.

---

[2] John Hume was co-recipient of the 1998 Nobel Peace Prize in 1998, with David Trimble.

When the SDLP's John Hume met Seagate executive Brendan Hegarty in a Los Angeles bar, the investment that resulted transformed the lives of thousands of people in Londonderry. [3]

---

[3] Actually, the Duke of Edinburgh pub, San Jose, California

Preface

All of these stories, put in letters, are true. Most names have been changed or omitted to protect the innocent, guilty and injured bystanders. There is no intent to cause offence or misrepresent. This book was only written to bring a smile. These are individual stories which are not in any sequence, or required to be read in the order Brendan chose them. As a reader, pick them in the order you would like.

The twenty stories are spread over five continents, Europe, Africa, South America, North America and Asia. Eighteen of the stories tell of unfortunate situations in which I have found myself. The other two stories cover places I have been which have suffered from unfortunate consequences. About half the stories are put into a workplace context but they are all really about people, not business. The intent was to write them in a humorous way.

The vast range of stories span life-threatening moments, sheltering from a riot, working out how not to bribe someone in Brazil and befriending a Gaucho in Argentina. Some are socially complex and some just highly embarrassing. All describe challenging circumstances. If I haven't made you smile, I should have at least given you a situation where you can think how you might have reacted. You'll probably smile then.

La Scala, Milan

1. "Well, Mrs. Clutterbuck, apart from that, how was the Opera?" Milan

Dear Brendan,

I've only been hit in the face once in my life.

It was very rare that Angela accompanied me on business trips. We're the sort of people that have never really been happy to mix business with real life. However, a business trip to Milan happened to be the day before Good Friday and we decided it would be a great idea to spend Easter weekend in

Milan as we had an empty nest at home and no commitments. This was going to be great.

On the Thursday before Easter, I had to travel north of the city to meet and speak to twenty-two Italian bankers who were interested in changing their business culture and wanted me to assess how we could help them identify the most influential and powerful people in their organisation. We had a software tool (a forerunner to Facebook in many ways) which could do that. The historians would be delighted to note that this was in 1994.

Angela was very happy to discover the art and fashion of Milan that day. I really wish I had joined her. As a surprise, I had booked two seats for the opera in the world-famous La Scala. I had made the booking via the concierge at our hotel for Good Friday. They were expensive and cost a bit more than I had expected (English understatement), but our concierge Guido explained that "At sucha shorta noteece meester, I hadda to pulla somma strings." I may not have paid face value.

The opera house is fantastic. It has a capacity of 2,800 people and, on this day, it was sold out. As we walked to the area where it's located in the city, it was obvious that this was not only a popular opera but a great day to see it. The opera was L'elisir d'amore (The Elixir of Love), a comedy, and everyone was clad in their best bib and tucker.

Entering the building, we both felt that we were in a very special place. The house had specially dressed ushers who would escort anyone requesting, or needing, assistance to their seats. Our seats were also special. If you look at the picture at the head of this letter, you will see the orchestra pit between the audience and the stage. To the left, we had the aisle seat and the one next to it, second row from the front. The seating matched the price and we were very happy. We had a great view of the stage, with almost everyone sitting behind us. Keep this in mind.

As we took our seats, the two seats directly in front of us (in the front row) were empty until the very last second as lights dimmed and the orchestra started. A man and women hurriedly sat down and immediately set about devouring each other in very passionate embraces. Arms, hands and heads were swirling around in a blur. This carried on for the whole of the first act except for very brief periods when they said something to each other in loud German.

At the interval, Angie and I decided to go outside for some fresh air! Interestingly, most of the opera audience also went outside for a break. Of course, this being Italy and in 1994, everyone went outside for a cigarette or short cigar. It was very pleasant standing outside such a beautiful place; however, a light rain began to fall and huge puffs of smoke billowed in our direction. This sent us back into the opera house to really soak up the ambience and tradition. It was truly memorable.

We took our seats again and waited for the second act. The two seats in front remained empty as the lights dimmed and the orchestra started. From nowhere, an usher dressed from top to toe in 16th-century Milanese attire showed an old lady, most probably in her early eighties, to the aisle seat directly in front of us. She had a thick stub of a closed umbrella, large oversized raincoat buttoned to the neck and white walking cane. It was obvious she was blind from the way she was guided fumbling and stumbling into the seat by the gallant usher. Angie and I, conscious of the off-Broadway act that had been going on in front of us before the interval, had exchanged hypotheses on the scenario. We agreed it was probably a naughty weekend of some sort, away from the hustle and bustle of car manufacturing in Stuttgart or high finance in Frankfurt and the rampant twosome had found their hotel and settled things properly. With the blind old dear now sitting in front of us, things were looking up. Or so we thought.

Around 3 to 5 minutes after the second act commenced, the luscious and bubbling German couple returned. The tall muscular German male shouted in a sharp, acute German accent,

"You! Vot are you doing in my zeet?!"

Our old lady said nothing. Her face was turned upward and, from what we could determine, she was on Planet Opera sipping from the cup of 'The Elixir of Love'. She didn't move. The upright and fuming German started getting impatient within about three picoseconds.

"Vot are you doing in my zeet?! You are in my zeet?! Get out of my zeet!"

By this time, the whole 2,800 people (almost entirely behind us and in direct line of vision), orchestra and players heard the kerfuffle and their attention was being drawn. Angie and I summed things up quickly. Our hero (me) quickly looked around for an empty seat and 3 rows behind us, but sadly across the central aisle, was one seat empty. I leapt into action. Our Italian, eighty-year-old, blind (and semi-crippled as I found out to my cost split seconds later) clearly did not understand English and certainly not with the German accent being barked at her. She remained calm and blissful. Our hero decided to act as her usher and tried to take her arm in cool English gentleman fashion and to guide her to her new seat. The next thing I knew, an umbrella, slightly dampened by the interval Milanese rain, hit me hard on the side of my face.

Undaunted by the current task at hand, I tried lifting her and caught her other hand as it swung into my ribcage. The two athletic Germans stood glaring at me as if I was to blame for everything. Angela, not one to hold back a comment when our hero didn't think he needed it, cried out,

"For God's sake, Paul, get her into the other seat now!"

I resisted a response. By almost giving the 'lovely' old lady a fireman's lift, I managed to pull, drag, yank and shove her the 20 feet into the utopia of the empty seat behind us. The Germans sat down with indignation. I stood pretty exhausted in the central aisle, slightly swaying and disoriented. 2,800 people, plus the aforementioned operatic staff, were staring. Luckily, Angie's sweet voice guided me back to my seat...
"Over here, for God's sake!"

I slumped down in my seat and closed my eyes for about 20 minutes and looked back to find our dear lady smiling, with glazed eyes, listening to the sweet opera belting out. Our new German friends were in a suffocating clinch.

On exiting, I asked the usher why he had put the lovely old girl in the seat. It appears it is a tradition that if a seat is empty at the start of the second act the poor, disabled or disadvantaged of the city are escorted to it for the remainder of the performance. "Besides," he said. "She is my aunt."

As ever,
Paul

PS: "Tradition is a wonderful thing," I said to Angie on the plane home, referring to La Scala. She didn't want to talk about it. Our hero sat quietly nursing a rather unpleasantly acidic Pinot Grigio and a rude welt on the side of his face which was still smarting from the umbrella bashing.

PPS: The Italian bankers (the purpose of the trip)

absolutely loved the consulting tool and the services offering along with it. However, as is the custom in Italy, to expose who is powerful and truly influential in an organisation would be impossibly dangerous. Equally, it would very dangerous to identify people in senior positions who made no contribution and whom no one respected. Not one bank bought the software or the consulting service which would have made it highly valuable for their businesses. My company was paid for my hard work that day plus travel expenses, but we did not get the business leverage I was seeking. C'est la vie, or "è la vita" as a La Scala usher would say.

Café Hegeraad, Amsterdam

2. The Small Frenchman Amsterdam

Dear Brendan,

I wanted to change my life entirely when I retired.

I knew that I should prepare for the one thing I had never had before; unstructured time to myself. At that point, Angie and I were lucky enough to be able to think about where to spend time in the winter months. However, we always kept in mind what Oscar Wilde said, "Never get sick in a foreign language," and with all my travelling I had understood the point entirely. That thinking was about getting the big picture of retirement organised.

The smaller picture needed detailed planning so we started thinking about a small set of projects. Apart from a series of travelling projects, I wanted something challenging, physically and intellectually, but also fun. I decided they should involve raising funds for the Operation Smile UK charity. It would be an attempt to show emotional support to my youngest grandson, Josh. The cycling and climbing Kilimanjaro 'projects' were mostly very physical challenges without a lot of fun but they have spawned their own stories which have made my list of letters for you. The 'Inside Amsterdam' cafés/pubs book may not make too many people's list as intellectually challenging projects, but for a dyslexic like me, it was like another mountain to climb. You know about the book, but I don't think you know too much about my research and initial selling escapades.

The research was punishing and hard work. No, really it was. I covered 80 cafés/pubs in order to settle on the 60 which made the cut for the book. I visited them during four three to four-day trips, starting on my rented bike at around 9:00 am and sometimes finishing the day around one o'clock the next morning. The interviews and discussions with owners, bar staff and customers were quite exhausting (no, really, they were) and sometimes intensive, but it was their hospitality that nearly did for me. Even those cafés I visited at 9:00 am would offer me a cognac with a coffee. I do realise that I could have declined, but my acceptance depended on whether it was an owner or bar staff, combined with what I guessed would be the value of the cafe to the book. I had to pace myself, but not shun the bonding that comes with a cognac. The most damaging visit was to the Ij Brewery where the Dutch, ex-pop star (1960s era) owner told me he was going to educate me in the history and products of his business. At the end of three hours, I was so educated I could hardly stand up. Some of his seasonal beer products were 13% alcohol.

In general, my research notes early in the day were good but scant the more the interviews and hospitable hosts accumulated. They were as readable as a doctor's prescription. Towards late afternoon they went downhill and then seriously downhill from early evening onwards. I had to revisit some the next morning to clarify what I had written and what I had clearly misunderstood. I learnt to construct the day's schedule according to my hunch on value. Venues such as the American Hotel in the Leidseplein area were respectable and I was treated like royalty with a free lunch and offers of a discounted room on my next visit to the city. Also, some agreed to me holding a book signing event in their bar area or café following publishing. I was overwhelmed by their generosity. For their part, they were astonished that an Englishman was interested in their café, its history, unusual people and events enough to write a book. You will remember that some of these cafés and pubs are more than 350 years old and almost unchanged. More than a few times I had my doubts that it would be worth writing the book or that I could actually complete it and raise enough funds for the charity to justify the effort. But to be honest, I just wanted to do it for fun anyway.

During September 2008 it was completed. I had a

marketing and selling plan which kicked off with a flying three-day visit with a hundred books in a rucksack and a rented sit-up-and-beg Dutch bike. Day one was a disaster. I had the first flight out of Southampton and a schedule which included a book signing event in a café on the Prinsengracht at around 6:00 pm that evening. Fog descended on the airport fifteen mins before boarding with departure delayed indefinitely. After two hours waiting for the fog to lift, I'd had enough. I found the airport manager, explained that I was an author (therefore, very important) about to undergo a book signing tour of Amsterdam for a charity and could he give me permission to start selling my book in the airport while we wait for the fog to lift. Surprisingly, not only did he agree to this, but he set up a table and chair in the middle of the passenger lounge and made an announcement over the loudspeaker system to everyone about the book I was selling and why. He must have thought it a useful distraction from the delays piling up and passengers getting agitated. I sold twelve books in the space of one hour, only two of which were to people hoping to fly to Amsterdam that day. The rest must have been really bored.

Eventually, the fog lifted and we took off. I arrived at the book signing café two hours after the scheduled time. They had given up on me even though I had left messages that I would be late. Never mind, I sold four books just hanging around the bar.

The following day went well with two book signings and around fifteen pub visits. Sales were going well and charity money was mounting. The next morning also started well and after lunch, I arrived at Café Hegeraad. It is the café on the front of the book and the photo inserted at the head of your letter. It has a reputation for argumentative and very 'local' customers. Personally, I like it because it is one of those cafés which feels like someone's front room and is unchanged in one hundred and fifty years. It also is proud to have the smallest Gents toilet in Amsterdam. I had a good chat with the owner who remembered me doing the research. He bought four books, one for his wife, one for his nephew, one for an old friend and one to keep in the bar. He tried negotiating on the price until I reminded him that he would be taking money away from children who needed facial surgery. Even a tight-fisted Dutchman finds it hard to come back from that line in defence of a price! It was a good visit and I sold two more books to customers sitting at the bar. During the visit, I had been conscious, much of the time, that there was someone behind me watching and listening to my conversations with the owner and other customers. As I packed my rucksack with the remaining books, I was approached from behind. The man standing there was easily less than four feet tall. He picked up one of my books and thumbed through it. After a few seconds, he spoke.

"I moost 'ave zis book!" I detected more than a wiff of a French accent. "Yes, of course. Thank you. They are €20 each."

"Boot I 'ave no mun ay."

"Oh, I'm sorry."

"Boot I aff too 'ave eat. Eat iz bootifull. Eat iz luv lee. I moost 'ave eat!"

"Well, I'm sorry, the money I am asking goes to a charity for children. I cannot just give it away."

I was feeling very uncomfortable at this stage. Most of the customers within earshot had stopped talking were listening intently and appeared to have knowing, broad smiles.

"I moost, moost 'ave a copee. Eat iz for meeee…!"

"Look, I'm sorry, I have to leave now."

I finished packing and left by the main door. I walked over to the railings around the large Noord Kerk (North Church) where I had my bike chained up. I heard the door slam behind me. The diminutive chap had followed me out. As I started unchaining my bike, he started saying all the same things over again. He could see I was unmoved no matter how tall he stood. He changed suddenly and used a softer, more chummy tone.

"Well, maybe we cud go to my 'ouse. Look down zis street beside zer café. You see zat 'ouse wiz ze tricolour flag outside?"

"Yes."

Sure enough, there was a French flag outside a typical gabled Amsterdam house about three hundred yards along the street next to the café.

"Zis iz where I leeve. Maybe we cud go to ma 'ouse and I give you some of my alcohol. I mak eat myself."

"Oh, is it wine, beer or something like that?" I said starting to feel a bit mean.

"No, eat iz joost alcohol. I joost mak alcohol." He could see I was getting ready to leave again.

"Well, er, maybe you cud come to my 'ouse. We drink my alcohol. We get drunk togezzer and zen you 'ave sex wiz me. You cud give me ze book then? No?"

Then it hit me. He was gay. He doesn't really want the book, it's me he wants! It was one of those awkward moments English people really don't like. Everyone in the café knew what was happening, but why would they let on? I could see two faces at the café window. They were curious to see the outcome of yet another ploy by their short neighbour. They were relaying events to the whole café.

Slightly stuttering, I managed to blurt out...

"Look, that is a very lovely offer but I have a book signing arranged in fifteen minutes at the American Hotel (it had happened the day before). Please go home and wait for me there. I'll be back in two hours. I'm looking forward to your alcohol."

I jumped on my bike and peddled hard for the far side of the Noordermarkt Square and on, ironically, to the safer haven of the red-light district on the other side of Amsterdam.

Until next week...

As ever,

Paul

PS: I have not returned to this cafe since.

PPS: A copy of the book was requested by, and lodged with, The Amsterdam Historical Museum.

PPPS: To date, more than 450 books have been sold, largely through the internet (Lulu.com, Amazon and Barnes & Noble) and my friend Peter McQuade.

PPPPS: The book has resulted in children having much needed facial surgery somewhere in the world.[4]

PPPPPS: I really did have fun.

---

[4] *In total, the book, plus bike riding challenges and climbing Kilimanjaro raised enough for 234 children to have surgery. The best thing I have ever done.*

Looking at La Defense from the top of the Arc de Triomphe

3. 100 Lebanese want to know my name
Paris

Dear Brendan,

I have never met anyone from Lebanon as far as I know. However, you will see why my name was important to about 100 of them by the time you finish this story.

This story concerns our European headquarters in Paris and its beloved position in the 1990s. My first ever business trip, in 1974, was with you. Well, my last ever visit to that organisation, some twenty-one years later, was in a role which would have been inconceivable to me then.

1995 was a pivotal year for the corporation.

Background

A new CEO was appointed in 1993 and he set about transforming our business. By 1995, he had been at work for two years and things were turning around. The company had almost halved the permanent employees, sold off businesses which were not in future plans and started leasing, rather than owning and maintaining, most of its real estate. These were just some examples of the major actions taken.

The next target for dramatic change was corporate restructure and decision making. We all know what that means; fewer people. Less middle management.

To set the scene for you, the new CEO was unusually tough. One of the many stories told about him concerned his first day. He turned up at 6:00 am in the New York headquarters and chose an office to sit in; not his, but someone else's. Start time in those days was 9:00 am. At 9.20 am the executive who normally dwelt in that office turned up. Somewhat surprised at someone camping in his office, he asked who he was and what he thought he was doing there. The new CEO politely informed him and then asked why he was late for work. Fumbling for an answer he was asked another question in quick succession. "…and what is it you do that helps the customer and, or, the shareholder?" I'm afraid our poor timekeeping executive fumbled again. The CEO fired him on the spot. This was witnessed by several people and word got around. The new CEO had set expectations of what was to come in the next few weeks in the corporate head office.

Two years later, he turned his focus on the European head office. It was at this time I was to learn a lot about national stereotypes. They all played out before my eyes over the next three months.

My Role

The UK company had been at the forefront of downsizing and restructuring for-profit and Dick, its Chairman and CEO, was well regarded. Along with you, and three others, Dick had made a huge, positive impact on my confidence to grow and survive. From 1991 to 1994, the UK company had gone from record losses to sustainable profit. He asked me to write a published paper jointly with Imperial College, London on the company's transformation. This I did with a brilliant person from the college. She protected me from my mild dyslexia. I helped her with the fundamentals of what happened, the reasons why and its effect on profit and people. It was published and used in communications with customers and the marketplace. Just as it was being printed, Dick was promoted and sent to the Paris based European headquarters. At that time the head of the European business was an imposing Italian heavyweight, Enzo Fabrini.

Shortly after this happened, I received a phone call asking me to run a project in Paris and to report as soon as possible following my project in Belfast. A meeting was set for me to attend. I didn't know who was attending. I was shown into the boardroom and, ten minutes later, Enzo Fabrini walked in. He was a big man, probably six feet four inches, with cold black eyes. I noticed that his tie probably cost more than my suit, shirt and tie put together. He explained that he wanted to cut the European headquarters down to fifty people and my job was to tell him how. I asked what the current headcount was and he mumbled, "Two hundred." This mumble was a clue I didn't pick up on until later. He also wanted me to describe the future role of the new, slim organisation. I would have access to anyone I considered relevant and any data I needed; I could recruit one other person from the European headquarters staff. For this, he gave me a shortlist of credible people who were going to be retiring shortly anyway so had no skin in the game. Fabrini gave me three months and set the date in his diary for me to come back to him personally and then the European Executive Committee the following day. I walked out into the cold February air and thought about how lucky I was to be handed this poisoned chalice.

Executive Interviews

The first action was interviewing all Fabrini's reporting executives who sat on all the European committees and to each, I asked my first question, "How many people work at EHQ now?"

Most of the interviewees were pompous, cunning and evasive. They would all make it as politicians I thought. You may recall that almost all of them were either ex-country managers promoted to a European position or were going to be new country managers when they returned to their respective countries. They were all wedded to the structure that gave country managers the most power in each country. The new CEO in New York was already enforcing a new system which had appointed worldwide executives for each industry and he had given them the ultimate decision-making authority, over-riding any country executive. In short, the current structure was toast. The new man in New York didn't see any value in the country executive role other than local law and political integrity (in the UK that was interpreted as 'responsible for bogs and brushes'). This led to some interesting and quite entertaining interviews when I visited some of the country managers, but more of that later.

The most important piece of information to come out of my executive interviews was the fact that not one of them actually knew how many people worked there. Answers ranged between two hundred and eight hundred. The VP of Personnel gave the nearest and largest guess — eight hundred. So I went to payroll. My accounting background told me that you'll always know who works somewhere by finding out who a company is actually paying. Not rocket science as they say. I recorded local French employees and overseas employees assigned to the Paris organisation. The answer turned out to be one thousand, two hundred and fifty. Well, there's a thing! To scale down from two hundred is one thing; from one thousand, two hundred and fifty is another. As Stalin was credited with saying, "One death is a tragedy, a thousand is a statistic." Luckily, I didn't personally have to deal with tragedy unless, of course, I was to get the chop at the end of the project and be a statistic.

Unsurprisingly, every executive I interviewed, except the American imports, considered the established 'sovereignty' of the country manager and their territory as valuable and the key to the future. I didn't know much about the current company politics as, by this time, I'd been working in and out of a diverse set of customers and territories for about eight years. I was both bored with, and fearful of, internal strife. However, I knew which horse I would back on this one.

My last interview in Paris was with Dick at his house, in

the evening He made it clear that this project was another test by the new CEO in New York to see who was on board with the new business model (and who was not). As we ate our Chinese takeaway Dick took my set of interview questions and tore them up. "It's really very simple," he said. "Show how you can get to fifty people and show how very limited local country management would be in the future." Country management needed the European head office and vice versa. With customers, we had a duty of care to ensure that what we recommended was in our opinion the right course of action and we always had facts to back it up even though, in many cases, they really didn't care, surprisingly. Here, a course of action was going to take place anyway and the project was intended to flush out who the obstacles were. However, I did have a duty of care. Didn't I?

Country General Manager Interviews

I asked my recruited European headquarters employee for the project, who was about to retire, to define and categorise all one thousand, two hundred and fifty people. His name was Jesus Bush (as far as I could tell he wasn't related to either). Jesus was a classic example of the flotsam and jetsam washed up on the shores of remote places in large organisations. He was originally from Mexico, assigned temporarily to a small project to do with headquarter systems development, or some such nonsense, between headquarters in Latin America and Europe. That had been twelve years previously and he'd married a French woman and settled in Paris. He was great, I liked him tremendously and he worked hard and conscientiously even though he was leaving soon.

With Jesus ploughing through some tricky categorisation

I caught my first flight to interview a country manager.

UK

Of course, there was a new CEO in the UK now that Dick was in Paris. The new man here was previously the Finance Director and he was appointed to the role much to the surprise of everyone, including him. Although ill-suited to the role, he had assumed all the kudos normally shown to the top executive of a country's business. We went through the first part of my structured interview concerning the current and future role of European headquarters, and he was scathing. He had too many scars and bruises not to miss an opportunity to stick the knife in and when I suggested that perhaps a much smaller number of staff of, say fifty, would be better suited for a role concerning EU law and politics he quickly dismissed this and proposed zero. "Each major country in Europe should report directly to New York with the smaller countries reporting into one of the four largest according to language — i.e. Nordics, Netherlands to the UK, German-speaking countries to Germany, French to the French with Italy picking the eastern Med countries like Greece, Turkey etc." I thought, hmmm, he had definitely not sniffed the wind on this one. Having four smaller regional headquarters wasn't quite what the main man in New York had in mind. Anyway, I faithfully recorded his idea. On the subject of the role of country managers, he was a little unsure. "I think the big boss in New York understands the value of a country executive," he said pompously. "He asked me to arrange for him to meet Princess Diana when he was next in London. I wasn't able to do it, but it taught me that he understands the value." That wasn't my conclusion from that little anecdote!

Always one for a joke, he said as I left his office "By the

way, I have a soft spot for the European head office. It's called a swamp." I had the feeling that he wasn't going to find the next few months very funny.

Germany

I've forgotten the name of the General Manager in Germany, but he was tall and imposing and his office had the best position and view of the company's Stuttgart site. He kept me waiting for an hour beyond our appointed time which made no difference to me. As I sat in the inner reception room of his executive suite (I had already passed through two other reception rooms to get there), I noticed the tasteful art on the walls. There appeared to be a Picasso, Magritte and other replicas everywhere and I couldn't help but compare the blandness of the UK offices with what I was seeing here.

I was shown into Herr General Manager's office. The two assistants with him shook my hand and left. We sat down and I couldn't help feeling I was being filmed for an educational video on how to overcome intimidation. He started slowly and carefully articulating almost no views of what role the European head office should play. He indicated it made no difference to him, his staff or his business performance so it could be as big or small as anyone else wanted. He just ignored it as he considered himself as the ultimate executive in Europe. Germany could make or break our European business performance. I think he was probably right, but his tone didn't quite fit with the new world that was being forced through. It was funny how national stereotypes were being played out before my very ears.

The interview was pretty boring and predictable and I didn't get much useful information until right at the end I asked the question about the value of a country general manager in a new management model of industry-aligned rather than country-based businesses. His poise disappeared. "Ah zo ve haff cum to ze real point! Let me tell you sumzing. I get der question vrom New York about ze azzets of our German company. Unt zey asked how much wass ze art worth. I know ze New York staff haff been walking around my buildings taking notes on wat ve haff. I know wat iz de game because I haff a friend in ze Zotherbys in New York and zey haff been told wat art our company wants to zell in ze next three montz." His face was getting redder and he started gently banging his clenched fists on his desks as he talked. As he sped through his sentences, he increased the speed of his desk thumping. "Ve haff zis art for many years and it iz owned by ze German business. No one can zell sis art except uz. I refuse. Go and tell zem in New York zat Germany is not zelling!!" I was beginning to think his understanding of my mission had got lost somewhere. "OK, you can leeve now," he gasped. As I jumped into a Stuttgart built Mercedes taxi, I had the distinct feeling that I was falling into a very big black hole something like a vortex. Who had picked me out for this job and what had I ever done to them? What was I thinking in saying yes to it…? and then I remembered that a choice was not offered. Welcome to the world of the 'pawn in the game' I said to myself.

Italy

I knew of the President and CEO of the Italian company from his previous position as President and CEO of Latin America. I had had a little exposure to him in my role based in Delaware. He was a big cheese and he knew it. Elio Ragusa was born in Ragusa, Sicily. The only other person I had heard of who had been born with the same name as a Sicilian town was Don Corleone from the "Godfather" book and films, whom as you may remember came from Corleone, Sicily. However, Signore Ragusa was very definitely not fictitious.

Interestingly, but not surprisingly, he was in favour of a strong and heavily populated European head office. His big chum was Enzo Fabrini, the previous boss of the Italian company and my current project sponsor. He said he saw value in the European head office allowing the countries to be creative and empowered to align themselves with the culture and business structures that were uniquely Italian. On the subject of the value and future of the country manager (whatever the title bestowed) brought him alive and animated as only highly emotional, intelligent and political Italians can be. Rising from behind his desk, with a flourish of grand gestures, he told me,

"The new big boss in New York knows exactly how strong, powerful and valuable my position is. He wanted to visit Italy but only to have a private audience with the Pope. He is a practising Catholic. Did you know?"

I didn't of course but I nodded knowingly. "Well, of course, I just made one phone call and..." he paused for effect, clicked his fingers in the air and continued... "I fixed it!" I was a one-man audience to an intensely dramatic performance.

However, I was getting a little alarmed about what real and useful information I was getting. The final report and presentation were going to be very short on facts. Facts were something that was bread and butter to every project I had undertaken with customers. What was I learning? And could I use it? I headed back to Paris for the last major country manager interview and to catch up with Jesus.

France

The French company was in big trouble. Huge losses and no action to correct its slide had led to the country manager being replaced six months earlier. The new man in the job wasn't playing ball with my set of questions and all he wanted to say essentially was that his job was very difficult and no one was helping him. He droned on about the ins and outs of restructuring and his ideas but he didn't show any signs any action yet. One thing was in his favour he told me, "Of course, I can now fire people from the company." I asked him to explain. It appeared that French employment law at the time didn't allow companies to lay-off people if the company was making a profit. The French company was not making a profit and he, therefore, had a green light to reduce his workforce. Following a couple of my direct questions, he declared that he was still getting plans put together to restructure. I left his office to see Jesus.

European head office

Jesus had been doing some really good work. He'd broken down the one thousand, two hundred and fifty staff into permanent employees (French) and assigned employees from European countries, the USA and other geographies. He had categorised them by industry sector or support functions such as manufacturing and IT. At last, I thought I can get my teeth into this! However, there was a category called "other" with about one hundred and thirty sitting, waiting for further definition.

"Who and what are these Jesus?" I said. He was a little hesitant and it was clear he either didn't want to say or he didn't know. He offered up that he thought twenty must be the

European executive team but he was at a loss to know who the others were. It was time to see the VP of Personnel.

After about twenty minutes of his cooing and mumbling over the Jesus Bush document, it was unbelievably clear. The VP had never seen such a simple way of looking at the EHQ staff. That was a shock to me. We got onto the tricky subject of the mysterious one hundred. More dancing and off-on-a-tangent discussion before he confessed that they were employees who no longer turned up for work.

"Pardon?"

"Well, in 1978 when Israel invaded Lebanon, we shipped all our Lebanese employees to Paris and gave them jobs in head office. It was our way of being a good corporate citizen in those days. What with death and retirement those employees, number about a hundred now." He sat back in his chair and waited for my reaction.

"OK, but where are they? What are they doing on the payroll? Do they ever come to work?" I had many more questions which were about to be fired in his direction.

"Well, one to two of that batch still have jobs which they like and do turn up and do good work. However, I believe most of them have jobs in Paris they like more (pause) such as taxi drivers or waiters." He could see I was finding this unreal by the look on my face (I could never play poker). After another pause, I spoke.

"Why don't we just make them redundant?"

"French employment law doesn't allow companies in France to fire people if the company is making a profit. Our European head office is a separate company registered in France and it adds a ten per cent to its costs and bills the countries it supports. It's not set up to do anything but make ten per cent profit." I got a Gallic shrug accompanied by a purse of the lips with a slight high-pitched exhalation. I left his office.

I had a 'come to Jesus' session back in my temporary office in Tour Pascale. "Ok Jesus, how much do you really know about these Lebanese." I was firm. Eventually, he told me that most French employees in the headquarters either knew or had heard it rumoured in one way or another. I had a solution mulling around my confused and bewildered head. "Why don't we transfer them to the French company and then release them as part of our plan to get to fifty?"

"Magnifique!" Jesus said in a Mexican accent. Knowing he would be long gone by the time this would be implemented.

Conclusions and recommendations

I fed back to Enzo Fabrini my findings, conclusions and recommendations. He was delighted by the reduction in numbers to around fifty, which included a sizeable reduction in his reporting executives. The majority of the reduction comprised sending assignees back home or to the industry businesses which were global and whose HQ's were either in New York, London, Stuttgart or Singapore. We transferred admin, finance and IT to the French company and likewise the 'awkward' one hundred. I didn't mention the strange Lebanese set up to either Fabrini or the executive committee. It seemed best not to!

He was less than pleased with my recommendation of redesigning the country manager role in line with the reduced European head office role and leaving them with just law and politics; whoops, I mean cultural compliance. Not my fight so I wrapped up, handed over the agreed plan to someone in the French company who was lucky enough to be called the

'Implementation Executive' and left Tour Pascale, never to return inside the building. Dick called me to say well done the following week.

I spoke to Jesus Bush by phone three months later. He was the happiest Mexican I'd ever spoken to, and they always sound happy anyway. He had started a small bakery business with his wife and it was going well as he used some of his mother's recipes for Mexican cakes and pastries and the locals in Montmartre were rather taken with something new and different. As we were finishing our chat he said, "Paul, you should know that there are about one hundred Lebanese who want to know your name."

As ever,
Paul

Notes

The new CEO in New York pulled off one of the greatest corporate turnarounds ever made. Although an American, he was knighted by the Queen following Tony Blair's recommendation for services to education in the UK. With wonderful irony, during his tenure, he had closed our own internal education centres in Brussels, New York, Rio de Janeiro and Tokyo. He then sold the real estate. The money was reinvested to pay for transformation costs.

Dick was fired by Fabrini, seven months after my project ended, for disloyalty. He'd flown to New York to tell the new CEO chapter and verse on how Fabrini was resisting the new management system of industry businesses in Europe. When he landed back in Paris from his New York trip his office had been cleared and he had a short chat with the VP of Personnel about the three-month sabbatical he had been granted allowing him to follow a new career.

When Enzo Fabrini left the company, he became Minister for Innovation and Technologies in the Berlusconi government.

Elio Ragusa, after joining another firm, was investigated for alleged insider trading in his new role.

Jesus Bush still has a bakery in Montmartre I believe, now run by his son.

I have returned to La Defense only once since. It was many years later during one of my charity bike rides when we happened to be staying in the Mercure, La Defense. I was with three other madmen. I pointed to Tour Pascale and told them that I had once spent three months working in the building in 1995. "Oh, what did you do there?" asked one. "I did a lot of talking and listening," I mumbled.

4. The Long Drop and Baboon Ridge
Rift Valley, Kenya

Dear Brendan,

There is a long drop toilet in Kenya that must equal any in the world for its view. It is perched on the cliff edge of the Rift Valley looking straight across fifty miles to the other side. It has no door. The cliff drops away to the valley floor about three thousand feet below. The first time I used it Carl, my friend and our host, gave me some good advice.

Looking out across the Rift Valley from the long drop

"Before sitting, clap your hands loudly. If there are any bats or rats down there then they will clear away pretty quickly. Look for scorpions, spiders and small insects too. Welcome to the wilderness."

He had advised against going anywhere else, despite my strong desire not to use the long drop. He gave me various reasons and they were good enough for me to overcome my fear of what might be beneath my bended knee and arched back. I won't go into some of the less than savoury aspects of the African food chain, suffice to say I decided that the long drop was definitely the best option available to my English sensitivities. Long drops are very efficient, odour free and a highly practical way of dealing with human waste. This one had round mud walls and a thatched top.

Looking left from the long drop towards Baboon Ridge

Part of its strangeness to a non-robust bloke from England was that, no matter what was dropped in it, the long drop made no sound. No splash, no thud, no tinkle, nothing. That alone takes a bit of getting used to. The long drop is sited in the grounds of Carl and his wife Judy's house which they named 'Rangi Saba' (Swahili for 'Seven Colours' meaning Rainbow). They had built the house during the 1980s. It has three bedrooms, with a large open plan sitting and dining room and a large separate kitchen. It is also twenty-eight kilometres from any made-up road, and fifty kilometres from Nairobi. They acquired the land from the local Maasai Chief. There had been a mix up in the deal-making when the chief thought he was getting Carl's wife Judy as part of the settlement. It was nearly a deal-breaker when Judy declined. Two other couples had built in this area with all three houses perched along the rim overlooking the magnificent Rift Valley. You need a Land Rover or equivalent to get from the made-up road to the house. In the rainy season, at times, it is very difficult to reach the house at all. However, from this wilderness, you can be in Nairobi within two hours (when it is dry).

Angie and I had met Carl and Judy in Amsterdam in 1978. They had moved there from the New York area. Our families became great friends and remain so.

The reason why I was there is simple. Carl had been the one to suggest climbing Kilimanjaro and my brother Peter and friend Mikey had wanted to do it with us. Unfortunately, Carl had to drop out through severe knee problems but he very kindly suggested we spend a week with him perched on the Rift to begin altitude adjustment; his house is about six to seven thousand feet above sea level. It was a great idea and gave us a good start.

A week in the wilderness with Carl was a truly unforgettable time for the three of us. Carl was using wind and sun to provide power with a generator for backup (not needed while we were there). Rainwater was collected and reused. The staff reused food waste for composting or feeding farmed animals close by. At night, with a torch, sitting on the long drop (after clapping very loudly) you can view the star splattered sky through the doorless opening. There is no light pollution there. I have never seen the night sky so clear and so full of bright stars. It was worth travelling there just for that. At night, at about eleven o'clock, the wind blows quite strongly up from

Sunset at 6 pm every evening of the year

the valley floor. It makes an eerie sound, similar to an ocean crashing against a shoreline. The sound stops abruptly around daybreak — six o'clock. This happens every night of the year. It troubled me for the first two nights but by the end of the week, I'd stopped noticing it. The house stands almost exactly on the equator so sundown and sunrise are at six, am and pm, every day of the year.

For the first three days, Carl had organised for the three of us to see and experience something local. The first trip was to an elephant orphanage. The occupants were young elephants who were found wandering alone in the bush or standing next to the dead bodies of their parents. Parents whose tusks were removed, not surgically but brutally, and sold on to lucrative far eastern or North American markets. The illegal hunters have a very tidy income from this business despite the laudable efforts of the government and local agents.

The second trip was to a school, way out in the bush. Carl had suggested this as a way of understanding a little bit of East African life. He took us through the bush, scrubland and dust plains in the land rover. The school had about 180 children with ages ranging between four and fifteen. They all, of course, walk to school. Some, we were told, from as much as five and six kilometres away. Given the terrain this was remarkable. Almost all the children had a school uniform and those that didn't, the parents had either forgotten to ensure the children put it on, or didn't care, or they had sold the clothes which had been provided through a government agency. All the children loved the uniforms and you could see how proud they were to have it. Parents were highly motivated to send their children to the school, no matter how far they would have to walk because the school provided a meal. Possibly, the only meal of the day. We were met by the headmaster and taken around. Carl explained that his mother, living in Tampa, Florida had stayed with him a few years previously and wanted to know how she could help the school. The headmaster had pointed out that there were no toilets for a school with 180 children and nine teachers. For a contribution of three hundred dollars, she had three long drop toilets installed with Carl's supervision. Being a resourceful headmaster, he very quickly pointed out to the three Englishmen in front of him that football was the boys favourite sport but it was embarrassing when other schools visited them to play. They had to use coats for goalposts. I looked at Carl who had a twinkle in his eye. A brilliant sting operation had been set up. I asked what help it was that the headmaster really needed in this area. So he said, "We need metal goal frames with goal nets." I agreed to fund it. He then looked at my friend Mikey. "And I'll buy some footballs." The headmaster didn't stop looking at Mikey. "Ten footballs…?" A kindly smile was beginning to form on the face of the headmaster. "OK, twenty footballs." He then turned to look at my brother who said, "I'm a blacksmith and would like to design and pay for something that the girls in the school would like. What would the girls like headmaster?"

"A large swing which six to ten girls could use together. They have a wooden one at the moment which is old, rusted through at the bolts and dangerous. They would like a new one."

My brother Peter said, "I will design it and pay for two and Carl can help by managing the production locally." Everyone agreed and everyone was happy... none more so than the headmaster! About two months after we had left Nairobi, Carl organised the production of the goalposts and swing with one of his staff acting as a local negotiator. The footballs were purchased but the trickiest supply issue was with the nets. They were a rarity in Kenya because they had so many other practical uses that they either disappeared through theft or their owners applied them to more pressing needs. I have seen photos only recently of the school where Carl's mum's long drops, my metal goal frames and Peter's two swings still stand. The nets and footballs were long gone.

As part of the school tour, we were taken to a classroom to speak to about thirty children. They were older and looked very smart in their uniforms. I was invited to say something so I stood at the front and told them that we were going to attempt to walk up Kilimanjaro the following week. Almost all of them were staring at my feet. They were fascinated by my climbing boots. I later learnt that a man's wealth in that part of the world can be assessed by what he wore on his feet. Although they were all very shy, I asked them if they had questions. They froze. So I asked them a question. "Does anyone know how high Kilimanjaro is?" Almost every hand shot up. The headmaster stepped forward and pointed to a boy who was probably fourteen years old. "Sir, it is 19,341 feet above sea level and the highest place in Africa." He was painfully shy and embarrassed but his headmaster looked at him with love and pride. It was a very beautiful moment; I will remember it for a long time.

One of the teachers at the school was a very beautiful lady named Florence. My friend Mikey was very, very taken with her and as it happened, she was the sister of one of Carl's staff at the house and also a daughter of the Masai chief from whom Carl and Judy had bought the land to build the house. Florence was in awe of Carl and Judy and had named her two children after them. A boy and a girl. She sold Masai jewellery that she made herself as a side-line and we all bought something — of course. She also invited us to walk with her through the bush to her village which was (sort of) on the way back to Carl's house. We saw an Ostrich and several largish, four-legged and fast Eland. A warthog ran across our path which was a track worn away by people walking in roughly the same direction for about two thousand years. We arrived at a small hamlet of mud huts after several miles and crossing a stream. How do people in these circumstances keep their clothes looking so bright, colourful and clean when they live in mud huts with dusty floors and a local stream to wash them in? Florence did not invite us to her home. She said, "My husband is at home. He will be drunk. I married a savage." We thanked her and started out in the direction she had told us and eventually we made it back to 'Rangi Saba'. It had been a great day.

During the first five days, we also did some walking around the area as part of our altitude climbing preparation. One of Carl's Masai staff, whose Christian name was given as Peter, also acted as a guide for our walks and, as I'm not a naturally brave nor an adventurous person when it comes to nature or the wilderness, I was very grateful for his guidance. Peter, my brother, however, is fearless and very adventurous. He was itching to take a different path from Peter our guide. Carl had told Peter our guide not to be too ambitious in our trekking. To us foreigners, he said to get back to the house way before sundown as it goes pitch black immediately the sun disappears. There was to be more than one reason for saying this. During these first few days, Carl would tell us of the different types of animals he had seen on or alongside his decking and grass patch at the back of the house, overlooking the Rift. The smaller types of predators (no Lions), medium-sized and small herbivores, reptiles (not aquatic of course) and a huge range of birds. He emphasised constantly the need to check our shoes, walking boots and any other footwear we had with us for scorpions and other slippery customers before slipping them on. This was definitely a different type of briefing compared to prancing along the Hampshire and Sussex South Downs Way to a pub for lunch and then home again.

I was starting to struggle a bit with the altitude, even at only six to seven thousand feet, so one of the days I declined to go with Mikey and brother Peter and Peter the Guide. They

Carl and I sat here for 8 hours "shooting the breeze"

set off and I sat with Carl for about eight hours just chatting, drinking wine and beer (very bad for altitude sickness) and soaking up the beauty around us. It was another type of great day. Brother Peter, Mikey and Guide Peter arrived before sundown and declared that they had walked down the side of the Rift to the Valley floor below and then walked back up. That's three thousand feet down and then back up. Thank God I didn't go with them.

The day before we were to leave, Peter the Guide wasn't available to help us. Brother Peter wanted to go out and do something anyway and I detected that he was pleased we weren't to be shepherded. "Don't go far and keep the house in sight the whole time," were Carl's final words as we set off to walk around and just keep active. We took a look round and my brother liked the look of an area to the left of the house which we hadn't discovered yet. After about an hour and half of walking down and along the side of a mountain — the house out of sight for at least an hour — we were at a point where below us the side of the mountain fell away and above was steeply banked upwards. However, there was a hill across from us which looked climbable and had a piece of flat land that bridged to it from where we were.

"That looks a great hill to climb to get a view. I wonder what kind of view it has. Let's go and find out." Peter the Adventurer had a gleam in his eye.

"No thanks. I'm not feeling so good and I'm not sure we have kept track of how we get back to the house," I said. "Why don't you and Mikey go and have a quick look and then I think we should start back."

They set off like a shot up the hill. I saw them get to what I assumed to be the top of the hill and then they disappeared. I sat down. Waited. I laid down and waited. I closed my eyes which helped with my altitude problem. It must have been half an hour and they still did not reappear at the top of the hill. I needed to pee. I found a place nearby, frankly anywhere would do as it was the wilderness. Having completed the relief, I sat down and waited. A minute or two later, a strange noise barked out. It sounded like a fierce dog. Then another very loud bark. After the fifth or sixth loud bark close by, I was starting to think something wasn't quite right. The bark sounded like a cross between a rabid, wild dog and a Tyrannosaurus Rex. Something, or rather somethings, were very angry and agitated. Then I saw a large male Baboon.

And another and then the best part of twenty. They spread around me, barking their heads off. OK, I had to make a decision. We were probably ninety minutes from Carl's house from where I stood. I had no idea where my brother and Mikey were. I was surrounded by a troop of angry, large Baboons who by this time were bearing their teeth. In about ninety minutes, it will be pitch black. The three of us are without question, in a very beautiful but highly dangerous wilderness; and we are separated. Carl actually had no idea which direction we had taken. This was not something we'd planned for.

The question of the moment was WHAT TO DO NEXT? My good old business training and human instinct told me not to move as the returning walkers would presumably come back to the last known place they had seen me. My survival instinct said — "Sod 'em, save yourself!" It was a dilemma.

A dilemma which, with Hollywood timing, was resolved. Just as my survival instinct was about to overrule my rational calculations, Peter and Mikey came back over the hilltop.

"Hey, Paul. Did you know you are surrounded by Baboons?" shouted my brother.

"YES. I f*****g do!!"

"But there must be about well over a hundred of them."

A very agitated and angry Baboon

"Peter, get back down here and let's leave before I'm sexually assaulted by all of them!"

They descended and I walked up towards them. It seemed better that we take the way out together than individually. As we left along the side of the mountain from the direction we

The light was fading fast on Baboon Ridge

came, the Baboons parted, still barking loudly, allowing us to depart their domain. The light was fading. We knew we had a very limited amount of time to get to Carl's house before darkness fell with a thud.

It had been dark for about ten minutes as we entered Carl's house. We had had his room lights to guide us. Carl is a very cool guy and did not appear to have panicked. He got us each a drink — cognac I think — and stood there looking at us with Peter the Guide and Christopher the Cook waiting for the story.

"Bwana Paul, you went where?" Christopher spoke with a very soft Swahili accent. I explained roughly where I think it was and told them the story. Peter the Guide hung his head. Christopher the Cook's eyes were as big as saucepans. Carl was calm.

"Are you familiar with the area we are talking about?" I asked.

"Oh yes, Bwana. That is Baboon Ridge. No one goes there. Very dangerous. Plenty Baboons. Maybe two hundred."

I expanded a bit on what had happened and when they heard that I had taken a pee there was a hiss of air sucked through teeth.

"Oh Bwana, male Baboons go up the hillside during the day and female Baboons go down the hillside with the babies. You pee pee between them? Not good. Male think you trying to take over troop and territory. Did they attack you?"

"As near to an attack as is possible without any actual

penetration," I half-joked. Carl laughed loudly. He said, "Did any of us mention Baboon Ridge? Hmm, maybe we should have, sorry. I'll put it in the guestbook briefing for the next time we have guests. I'm glad it all worked out."

The next day we travelled back to Nairobi airport and boarded our plane for Arusha, Tanzania, the nearest airport for Kilimanjaro. As we flew there, we passed Kili just as night was falling and there were some angry clouds and colours and a rather foreboding, enormous mountain grew out of the huge, flat plain. This sight was breath-taking and enabled me to finally forget those words spoken to me by my brother...

"Hey! Paul! Did you know you're surrounded by Baboons?" However, I love him very much.

As ever,

Paul

Kilimanjaro from the air – looking easy to climb, it isn't

5. The best Uzbek restaurant in Tashkent

Dear Brendan,

It was 3 am, 14th July 1998 and I looked out of the aeroplane window at the moon reflecting off the Caspian Sea and wondered just how it happened that I was there.

My new colleague Brian James had called me on the previous Friday and asked if I would stand in for him during the next two weeks on all customer calls whilst he was on holiday. He said it should be a fairly low-key period, he had only just joined us from one of our competitors and his role and scope were still being defined. Or so I had been led to believe.

The following Monday Jo, my secretary, came into my office with a worried look and a large amount of paperwork, tickets and reading material. "I've got your tickets for Tashkent and all the preparation material you'll need for the meetings," she said in as much of a matter-of-fact way as she could.

Naturally, I laughed loudly. She continued, "No, really, seriously, I have. What's wrong, why are you laughing?"

I had either been stitched up like an oven-ready turkey or my new colleague had been ambushed by some cunning account manager of a remote territory or both? I learned later it was both. An Austrian, from our Vienna office which had acquired new territory authority over our Russian business and the old Soviet satellite countries had organised the visit. He needed to show some initiative and getting someone from London to visit must have ticked a few of the objectives his boss had set him that quarter. Official meetings were set up with the newly appointed CEO's of the National Bank, and Central Bank of Uzbekistan. Also, a vague reference to a meeting with Uzbek Government Officials. I was to travel the following night and return Saturday. Hotel and travel had been arranged and I would be met at the airport and would be escorted to the customer meetings throughout the week. We had three clear business objectives I was informed and, at some point during the week, they would be revealed by my Austrian colleague. It became obvious on the plane over, whilst looking at the moon's reflection on the Caspian Sea, that Brian had fled on holiday not knowing how to deal with an aggressive salesman in a corporate culture he did not yet understand and he'd felt I was probably the best person to handle the situation given my longevity and survival record. Some people call it teamwork, but I felt I had done the wrong thing for the right reasons. I had "taken one for the team" involuntarily. However, I should have known better.

I looked away from the moon's reflection and set about reading my brief about the country, the opportunity and the potential customers. It sounded almost like a normal business trip. Later the following week, my boss would to try to console me with 'pioneering in emerging markets' and 'doing what is expected' coupled with 'you're a great team player'. All highly debatable points, as you will see as you read on.

Uzbekistan in 1998

When the Soviet Union collapsed and dissolved in 1991, bona fide Russians mostly went back home or, if second generation, their parent's home country. Russians had been the ruling elite in pretty much all the satellite countries, including Uzbekistan, and this had had a special effect on business and government that I had not thought about nor experienced before. No one knew how to make a well thought through decision. No previous decision-making processes or leadership remained and subsequently, people who rose to power either tried to emulate the ruthlessness and autocracy that had gone before or a weird form of democracy was installed where everything was discussed, openly and frankly, which of course hadn't happened before. Consequently, no one felt confident enough to risk a decision. Nor had anyone set up a management system in which decisions could be taken collectively with confidence. Russia had ruled this part of Central Asia since the 1850s. During the 1930s, Stalin purged and executed the entire leadership of the Uzbekistan Republic and replaced them with Soviet (Russian) officials.

That Russian leadership had been sustained until the Soviet Union imploded in the early 1990s. Uzbeks had tried to establish their own democracy in the following six years with the 'help' of some rich individuals.

The other major factors pertaining in 1998 were the huge untapped natural resources. Minerals, oil, gas and precious metals (it is the 7th largest producer of gold). The Soviet system was highly inefficient at developing the satellite countries. One theory was that inefficiency helped control them and kept their power limited. This meant a huge commercial opportunity for experienced, western companies and governments to help grow their economies. Business in the country was embryonic and inadequate compared to the world in which it was forced to trade. It needed help and our company wanted to be part of that help in the short, medium and long term. I was to discover that my four days there were meant to be the start of the beginning.

Day 1

I landed in the dead of night and went through passport control and customs even quicker than if I had arrived at a small Greek Island. I was met by two people at the airport. One who introduced himself as my "chauffeur" for my stay and the other chap was introduced as my bodyguard. He didn't speak to me but was eyeing me up and down like the Schwarzenegger terminator, registering height, weight and fitness levels. He shouldered a weapon. They took me to the Intercontinental Hotel, Tashkent, for the rest of the night. I realised in the morning that they had slept in the car, outside the hotel, all night. Perhaps they would shower after they had dropped me off I mused.

My first stop was our Uzbekistan head office. We went via a very curious highway. Six lanes in each direction. The two outside lanes were for official government cars (Russian black Zil cars) only. The middle two lanes were for everyone else, including us. The two inside lanes were for small businesses, for example, a two-man garage set-up; a small grocery; a florist; a children's toys stall; a balloon salesman just standing there in the lane of the highway with thirty or so clustered above his head. Cars would pull off from the middle two lanes to get an oil change, buy a balloon or some flowers. I was amazed.

Eventually, we pulled up to a bombed-out looking building that was a brick and mortar garage and I ask why we had stopped. "Here mister" pointed my chauffeur to the second floor. There was a hand-painted hardboard sign with our logo. I was shown around the back of the garage to bare concrete stairs, without handrails, and arrived at our Uzbekistan head office.

As I entered, a young boy about twelve years old came quickly to greet me. He was dressed in clothes about two sizes too big for his small frame. He had a strong Mongolian look to him (Historical note: Genghis Khan and his Mongol army drove through this part of Asia in the thirteenth century).

"Harro, Sir. Mister Crudback?"

"Er, yes."

"Harro, Sir. My name Jumpshit. I am to meet you. Very pleased." (Yes, you guessed — I paused at the name.)

"Er, let me make sure I can say your name properly. Did you just say 'Jumpshit?'"

"Yes, Sir."

Another pause. Humour can sometimes break the ice a little. I wanted to say something that I thought would be hilarious. Somehow, against all my natural instincts, for once I didn't. Silence. No ice broken. I quickly moved on.

"I'm very pleased to meet you too Jumpshit. I believe we have several meetings set up over the next three days." I went over the agenda I had been given. "So can I meet the account representative for the first meeting please?"

"Yes, sir. That me. Jumpshit."

Hmmm. "Ok. What about the executive responsible for banking?"

"Yes sir. That me."

"Marketing?"

"Me."

"Is there anyone else here from our firm?"

"Well, sir. For now, I only Uzbekistan man. I cover all, very busy. But later we have two mens from Moscow, man from Austria and woman from local here to help with you."

More pause for thought. "Do you mean to say there is no one else employed by us in Uzbekistan but you?"

"Yes, sir."

"Right. So who are the men from Moscow?"

"Mens come every time we have big meetings with banks and government. Moscow office always look after us before Soviets moved out. Company wants same control they said me."

"OK, are they the same men each time? Do they have experience with banking and government business?"

"Same mens but no experience."

"I know I might be sounding a bit strange to you with my questions but who is the local woman?"

"Yana Varushkin. She will put your English to Russian and Russian to English all at same time as speaking."

I tried to be helpful and I was beginning to like Jumpshit. "We say 'simultaneous translation'. Well, she sounds like she will be very helpful to us. So let's get started."

"OK, but we wait for mens from Moscow. Yana Varushkin is waiting, already near."

The Muscovites turned up an hour late. They had stayed in the same hotel as me but were not assigned a chauffeur or bodyguard and they had tried to get a taxi. Russians were not feared and certainly not well respected anymore and apparently struggled to get anything they wanted. A taxi driver apparently can spot them a mile away.

"Good morning. My name is Viktor Smolenski." He was a small, dark-haired and pale-skinned man with small black beady eyes, a long, pointed nose and oversized ears. In summary, rodent-like.

The second Russian said nothing, did not introduce himself and was not introduced by anyone else. He had the same colouring as Viktor but was taller and quite plump. He wore a long, light grey, grubby looking raincoat that most people in the West would regard as a 'flashers mac'.

My patience was worn thin and I was very restless. I wanted to get on with the customer call. We went down the handrail-less concrete stairs and sure enough, my chauffeur and bodyguard were there waiting. We all got in and just as the door was closing, Yana Varushkin climbed in.

Yana was very softly spoken and her English was impeccable. I'm normally hopeless at guessing people's ages but I'd say she was about 35 (ish). She had a petite frame that was skin and bone with a complexion as white-as-a-sheet. She had large, very dark lines under her eyes and was slavic looking. In short, she looked like she had been hidden away in a dark place for a long time. She explained that everything I said would be faithfully translated and any questions directed at me she would put to me in English.

We entered a large, unattractive office block somewhere in the city. It was occupied, but not owned, by the National Bank of Uzbekistan (NBU). Ownership by 'private' companies was not yet allowed. This bank was supposed to be a private bank but the government owned thirty per cent and the rest was split between two private citizens, rumoured to be rich government ministers. Soon to be richer, no doubt.

From my briefing papers, my objective was to establish a small project to assess what priorities for change the bank had and be in pole position for the anticipated economic growth and dealing with the west. This project would be completed when we delivered an agreed set of business change priorities with a plan to achieve them. Sounds good.

The meeting room was hot, humid and airless. No air conditioning with no opening windows. Our team waited to be joined by the CEO of the bank. She walked in with an entourage of around twenty people. I say around twenty because some immediately walked out with others joining the meeting simultaneously. This constant flow in and out of the room by bank employees continued throughout the next one and a half painful hours. The CEO was a short, dark-haired and overweight woman who emitted large amounts of charisma and testosterone, with a side of perspiration. She introduced herself, as it happened only to me, in a heavy Russian accent. "Ludmilla Timoshenko," she roared with a look that told me she took no prisoners. She then sat down with a thump. Almost immediately the mysteriously missing man from our Austria office walked in - late! He walked up to me and introduced himself ignoring my new best friend Ludmilla. "Hi, I'm Manfred Remus. Pleased to meet you. How ya doin'?" Too many of my long-held values about how to handle situations with customers were being violated… and he was speaking in a horrible American / German version of English as though it were 'cool'. I didn't think it was cool. Questions were being asked in my head. What the hell was I doing here and would it be possible for me to survive this day, let alone another two?

So here I was, going through my standard introductory talk about how we approached business transformation projects. [What success and failure there had been and why; the quality of people we had; and how long an initial project might last]. Throughout, I was translated simultaneously which was slightly unnerving. I was constantly interrupted by bank employees, via my translator Yana Varushkin. The boss, Ludmilla, asked no questions. All of my team sat still and seemingly alert. The man from Moscow whose name I still did not know sat in his dirty raincoat and dozed. Most of the questions to me were trivial and seemed to be asked to impress Ludmilla. She sat motionlessly and hardly blinked. After about an hour into my thirty-minute presentation, I had covered everything. As is normal, now was the time to test her understanding so I started to gently ask Ludmilla some clarifying questions about the bank's ambition, timescale — you know — the normal stuff.

This threw the room into a little panic. My team was horrified and Ludmilla looked off guard. Jumpshit and Manfred reddened. I learned later that for various reasons it was not customary to ask the boss questions, something that was missed from my briefing. Again, I was angry about how we were treating the customer but Manfred from Austria assured me (later) that there would have been many things that Ludmilla would not have understood and not to worry about it. The point was that to ask her questions would bring her standing into doubt. Culturally, it was a direct challenge to her authority. She stood up, shook my hand said, "Spasibo!" (Thank you.) She left and every one of her entourage followed her out the door. So I was left in the hot, airless room with Jumpshit, a twelve-year-old from Uzbekistan, Manfred a large, overweight and sweating Austrian, two wordless Muscovites (one of whom still looked asleep in his dirty flashers raincoat) and my interpreter Yana who, in my judgement, was the only one in the room that last hour or so who had earned their pay, including me.

Manfred asked that we all remain in the room while we talk about the next two days meetings. I wanted an assessment of this meeting we'd just finished, what was achieved and what steps we should take next and refused to move on. Manfred tried to placate me and assured me that the meeting surpassed his expectations and that he could tell Ludmilla was delighted with what she had heard. Depressed, I stayed until we had properly prepared for the next two days. Manfred took the lead at last and I felt we had prepared as well as we could, given the really strange environment.

I returned to the hotel with my chauffeur and bodyguard, ate some supper and crashed out until breakfast. My driver and guard had stayed in the car all night again, but they now smelt considerably better I have to say. Things had to be looking up.

Day 2

I'd requested to talk to Manfred alone, first thing. "Who are these men from Moscow!?" I opened the discussion rather directly.

"Ah, yeah. Well, every time we have a customer meeting in one of the 'Stans', we have to have a minimum of two people from our office in Moscow join us as they still consider it their territory even though they have no business objectives or reporting structure relationship. They think they will get all this territory assigned to them in the next year or two so they invest time and money in keeping in touch. By the way, they insist on having copies of everything you have shown today so they can file it with their trip report and give a copy to the customer."

"No. We don't give away intellectual capital. Not to customers and not to non-practising personnel. It's not that we are precious about it. This content would very useful to our direct competitors and I can assure you the minute you give it away, you lose impact and its sense of value. Anyway, what actual job do these men hold? One of them doesn't even speak and the other one doesn't even stay awake when the customer is present! Are they something to do with the KGB?"

"But they will demand a copy." He ignored my question.

"Unless they are the secret police and will kidnap my whole family and torture them in dark cellars, they can get stuffed."

Manfred fell silent, unusually.

"Also, how come Mr Uzbekistan is a twelve-year-old boy?"

"Haha. You English sense of humour. Ya, he does look young, but he is already twenty-two. We have him appointed because his father is a big man in this country. He is wealthy and knows just about every important person in business and government. He can get us access to just about anyone we want, at any time."

"OK," I said. "But unless they are ready to do business this is all like knitting fog. They don't seem to be ready for our business to me, certainly not to make a business transformation project. You have to have some substance in order to transform it. Manfred, they don't even have electricity in half their bloody branches! How can you transform their banking system with our products and services when it will take a few years to get a baseline in standard banking practice and drag them into the twentieth century when the rest of the world is about to enter the twenty-first? They are going to need electricity."

We had a full and frank discussion about having basic knowledge, skill and information technology operating in this bank before tackling the more complicated capabilities of changing a whole or at least large parts of their operation. I knew he had specific objectives, which he would be paid on, that included projects such as this, whether the customer needed them or not. I was determined to help him as much as I could, knowing that it was not a good fit and that, in my opinion, poor use of our scarce resource.

The morning with the Central Bank of Uzbekistan went almost the same way as the previous meeting with Ludmilla's bank except for two things. All the customers were men, and Manfred was very good at schmoozing them. Our Muscovite non-speaking colleagues sat in the room again (one asleep in a dirty raincoat) and the bank CEO didn't seem to have a clue what I was talking about, even though my pale and wan interpreter Yana did a sterling job again. If I hadn't been thick-skinned, I would have started to lose confidence. We left with Manfred exuding happiness that we had "Hit ze spot." The afternoon wasn't to be so, how should I say this, successful.

Jumpshit told me we were to visit the Bankers Association of Uzbekistan and let slip that it was at their strong request that someone from my part of the company should visit them as soon as possible. They needed our help. This had triggered, he said, the original request back to London. As it happened, and in the end, that meant I ended up the fall guy.

So we all set off. Me, Jumpshit, Manfred, our two dumb, grubby colleagues from Moscow and Yana Varushkin. She was looking bulimic and frightened. We arrived at a site somewhere in Tashkent. It was beautiful. The garden had flowers (unusual) and magnificent sycamore trees. The trees had plaques stating that they were under the protection of the state. I was amazed. The building itself was a single-story, well-kept and almost art deco in design. We entered and were escorted through to what would be widely called a board room in the western world. Wood panels, leather furniture and plush Uzbek carpets. The finest silk Uzbek carpets. I smelt money. A smell I had not noticed since I arrived in the country.

The room had a huge old oak table that could seat at least twelve people either side with a couple of people at either end too if necessary. It seemed to be made from one piece of wood. We were ushered to one side with the other vacant. I had to sit in the middle of our side with Yana Varushkin next to me one side, and Manfred the other. The two snow-on-their-shoes boys sat our side but left a gap between us and them. Jumpshit sat at the other end of our side, but away from us. We waited fifteen minutes in almost silence despite me trying to get some sort of easy ambience or team spirit bubbling. If in doubt that's what I like to do. A nervous reaction to tension. Nobody in our team seemed to know why we were there. Why?

At last, a smallish man entered with a largish man in tow. He spoke Russian and shook my hand. Yana did not interpret. He indicated that we all sat down. He sat down directly opposite me and began speaking. Yana did not interpret. He spoke for about ten to fifteen minutes without a break and looked directly at me without diverting his gaze. I don't know if you have ever had someone speak to you in a foreign language for ten to fifteen minutes without anyone helping you understand what the dickens was going on but it's very difficult. How should I behave? Should I give a slight smile of warmth? Nod knowingly? Be stone-faced? I looked once at Yana who averted her gaze to a spot somewhere on the blank white wall opposite and fixed it there until the gentleman had finished. Yana then said...

"Mr. Dilshod Karimov would like me to summarise. On behalf of the Uzbekistan Peoples' Republic, the city of Tashkent, the peoples of Tashkent, the business community of Uzbekistan..." (etc., etc.) she went on and on. It nearly took a full ten minutes or so to summarise which was once again a testament to Miss Varushkin's linguistic ability. I got the message that this was just the bloody greeting. Thank God it went silent. My turn.

"Mr. Karimov. I would like to thank you for your most kind welcome and warm greeting..." (etc., etc.) I just made it up as I went along. Yana worked at double speed. As I talked, I remember feeling like it was an east meets west, Nixon versus Brezhnev peacekeeping conference. I lasted about three minutes in response which I thought was totally inadequate at the time, but on reflection that evening in the bar, Manfred said it was 'outstanding' and worth a 10 rating. In what? I thought; technical content or artistic impression? Neither seemed to apply.

Then Mr. Dilshod Karimov launched into the history and status of the Bankers Association of Uzbekistan. It was excruciating. He started to trail off, and Yana was not even breaking a sweat. After fifteen minutes, it turned nasty. He pointed aggressively to the corner of the room. There, unlit but immaculately clean, was one of our company's original personal computers, produced in the mid-1980s. It had to be at least twelve to fifteen years old. He said that he had requested my attendance because this computer had gone 'wrong' and he wanted me to fix it. Well, I'm not the sort of chap who can change the proverbial lightbulb with any confidence. I asked politely what Mr. Dilshod Karimov thought might be 'wrong' with it. He turned to the large man next to him who had sat po-faced throughout the proceedings. He looked directly at me, took a deep breath and gave us the diagnostic. He was the IT technician as it turned out and went on and on, of course, about what had happened, how he had tried all kinds of techie deft touches but had failed to rouse it from its slumber. When he eventually stopped talking, I turned to Jumpshit. He looked even younger than twelve. "I want you to make this a priority to either fix this PC or offer a significant upgrade for as little as you can charge without heavy company boots trampling on your head. I want you to explain and commit to that please and then ask if there is anything else you can help with. If not, we are leaving. Please thank him on my behalf for his time, patience and continued commitment to us." That was it. We left.

Back at the hotel, I had another little chat with Manfred. "Look, Manfred, I just want to know one thing and then I'm going to my room. What is Yana Varushkin's story?" I had decided while riding through the dusty and bleak streets back to the hotel to minimise just about everything while I was there. But I was still curious about Yana. Yet again, she was the only one to cut the mustard that day.

He paused, thought hard and then said, "Her father was a Soviet Red Army General based in Moscow. He was a very big deal. She learnt English through her father's position and was groomed to be a spy in the West until the Berlin Wall collapsed and with it the Soviet Union. Her father and mother were killed by people seeking revenge for the internal abuse and torture by the Red Army of their loved ones during the hard fist of the communist culture and the KGB tyranny. She fled, eventually arriving in Tashkent to hide and be safe. Her English is her only ticket out of starvation and further abuse. She lives alone in a small apartment in the city. No one has been there except me. I have been her main contracted employer for the last four years. She invited me, early in our relationship, to her apartment thinking that was the only way she would get the job. I'm not interested in girls so she was lucky. She is, as you will have noticed, very good so she got the job. No more story, my friend, that's it. She is a victim of circumstances like the rest of us."

"Thank you, Manfred. No more questions. Goodnight."

Day 3

I'm going to be leaving tonight! I checked my flight. Ugh. 03:45 am. Tashkent to Zurich then change for London. Ugh. All I had to do today was present to an audience of government officials our company's credentials, how we went about our business, what value we could bring to them with some case studies on what we have achieved. A piece of cake. Standard fare. It was going to be a good day. I could not get an internet connection, a mobile phone signal or the ability to make a phone call to Angela all week. Normally, I'd call at least once on any trip just to keep in touch.

As we entered the Government building, I could see some snow-topped mountains in the background that probably acted as a natural barrier between Uzbekistan, Kyrgyzstan and China. It was very picturesque.

Not so picturesque was the collection of odds and sods in our team. I still had the full complement in tow. As the large room filled up with a contingent of government officials I noticed something very unusual. The faces before me were the most diverse I had ever witnessed in one room. I had Chinese, North Koreans, Mongolian, Turkish, East German, Afghan, Pakistani, Indian, Arabic and Russian faces staring back at me. I only learned the full range of identities after the meeting. I could understand why most of the ethnic origins from the neighbouring countries were there. For many centuries, people migrated either normally as a way of life or through economic necessity. However, the East Germans were there as a result of Stalin's deliberate policy of moving people around to dilute ethnicity, particularly where they had a strong cultural identity. He apparently forced migration from East Germany following World War II as a way of weakening local power and instilling fear. The North Koreans had fled their regime but settled outside of China. Uzbekistan was seen as a safe haven for them. China not.

I was welcomed with the full introduction "On behalf of the Government of Uzbekistan, The Peoples of Uz..." (you get the drift by now) by what must have been a very senior member of the government judging by the fawning performances of Manfred, Jumpshit and Viktor Smolenski. Viktor's mate from Moscow had already settled down in his chair in preparation for his nap, coat untidily fastened at the neck.

I started my routine with Yana Varushkin translating as if her life depended on it (it probably did now I think of it). I slipped in all my usual early jokes to test the audience, which is usually received well by all nationalities. This time, however, it could be called stoney ground. I played it straight after that, thinking it's not long until it's downhill to the

Lufthansa refreshments. I had lots of questions and the session was quite matter-of-fact and low key. Actually, pointless would be a better summary.

I left with Jumpshit, my bodyguard and chauffeur. They were back to smelling rank. I invited Yana to join us all for dinner. She looked very worried about the prospect and declined, saying goodbye. Manfred said he would meet us at the restaurant; the men from Moscow wanted to come too.

"Ok mister Paul. It is your last hours here so where would you like to eat?" asked Jumpshit with genuine interest.

My next few words have stayed with me ever since. I said, "Jumpshit, I would like to eat in the best Uzbek restaurant in Tashkent."

I have always liked to try local food and drink on a first visit anywhere and I'd been cocooned in my hotel each evening from Tuesday. I had checked out, my bags in the boot of the car and I was demob-happy.

"Well, maybe we should try Turkish food tonight mister Paul."

"Well, no Jumpshit, I'd like to try Uzbek food tonight please."

"I know good Chinese, Indian or German food mister Paul."

"Jumpshit. The best Uzbek food, please!"

He shrugged and spoke to my chauffeur. We then toured half of Tashkent. The late afternoon, early evening was hot, around 40 degrees C (104 degrees F) and heavily humid. A thick, wet mist descended. As we drove, I noticed again that there were no street names visible. Manfred had told me that the Russians didn't want street names displayed as it would help foreigners or invading armies. Something that I remembered was quite normal in wartime Britain. We eventually came to the huge Chirchik River which flows 100 miles through Uzbekistan and into Tashkent. We parked and walked down the side of the steep river bank to a small building with a large patio where sets of tables and chairs were laid out. It was situated almost on the edge of the river. The Chirchik was wide, fast running and dirty brown. The sun was setting behind the drenching mist. I looked for the entrance to the building, but Jumpshit indicated that we were to sit outside at the small wrought iron, umbrella-less tables. I looked for something to dry my chair but my nameless bodyguard had moved ahead of us with a small hand towel and dried where I was to sit. It looked like the towel was marked 'InterContinental' and may have come from my hotel reception men's toilet. The toilet had a shower too so my driver and bodyguard's habits started to become obvious while they were on duty at my hotel. Keeping clean and fragrant depended on who was on duty behind the reception desk. Friend or foe?

I sat looking at the river and waiting for a menu. The mist was drenching me and it started to rain. It was clear that we could only sit outside. I looked hard at Jumpshit.

"The best Uzbek restaurant in Tashkent, Mister Paul." He shrugged a polite young shrug, but it was a shrug nonetheless. He wasn't old enough to give me a wry smile.

"OK, do they have a menu and maybe some wine?"

"No Mister Paul. Just one special dish at this restaurant and no alcohol, remember Uzbeks are Muslim."

"What can we drink?"

"Fanta. Do you want lemon or orange?"

"Bottled water maybe?

"No, just Fanta."

I ordered a Fanta and looked at the river. It was getting dark quickly. As the light faded, I noticed small but quite bright lights in the water. Some out in the mainstream, some close to the riverbank. I then noticed three men scooping the water. Further away from me were two other men who looked like they were hitting something with a club. Whatever they were hitting, another two were collecting them and taking them to a large oblong table close to a barbecue area. At this table, men were skilfully skinning the catch. I realised that after skinning the catch, it was popped on the large grills. Scales fell from my eyes just as a man from the barbecue came straight to our table with a plate of meat. No salad, vegetable or sides. It dawned on me that it was a river rat. Large, beady-eyed river rats. The lights were eyes! I looked again with immediate panic at the riverbank scene. There they were: very large river rats. Head off, tail off, filleted. The compulsion to retch was severe. Jumpshit, Viktor Smolenski, dirty raincoat man from Moscow, my driver and bodyguard all looked at me.

I said, "Come on, we all should eat as they bring the dishes to us so please, dive in!" Dirty raincoat man dived in. This was the quickest and most alert I had seen him all week. They all kept diving in as the rat production process brought plate after plate.

"Please, mister Paul, you must eat," pleaded Jumpshit. I tasted a lump of strong gamey meat with a small mouthful. Everyone except Jumpshit and me devoured the six platefuls put on our table. I asked my driver to take me to the airport. I said good-bye to everyone, including the Russians, and left with my bodyguard also in tow. Manfred hadn't joined us.

The airport was minimalistic. I asked if there was a club

lounge. Thank God there was. The taste of the best Uzbek restaurant in Tashkent was still in my mouth and even the three beers and a white wine did not help. I wanted food and the only items available were pretzels. The food on the plane helped and I slept all the way to Zurich, changed planes for Heathrow and arrived home around lunchtime. Angie greeted me asking, "How was your trip? Boring as usual? I didn't hear from you so I guessed things went well".

So I told her every detail of how boring it was.

As ever,

Paul

Notes

The company grew rapidly selling hardware and software over the next five years. Our Uzbekistan office moved from above the bombed-out garage to a more opulent building that had running water. Today, the firm's business advertising now includes the following statement: "Electronic service requests can be submitted for hardware or software under warranty or with a support contract." Electricity is now widespread.

Our office in Austria, assigned to look after the 'Stans', was disbanded. A newly created Russian Federation, located in Moscow, now runs the business which includes countries such as Uzbekistan.

Manfred Remus was given voluntary redundancy when the Austrian office was closed.

I have no way of knowing what happened to Yana Varushkin. The only one to earn her pay that week.

As far as I know, the best Uzbek restaurant in Tashkent is still in business.

Brian James, the new chap who had given me this opportunity, left our company in 2001 and re-joined the competitor he left for us. In 2002, we acquired that company and he rejoined our business but left soon afterwards. It's a funny old world.

A year or two later, I found out that "Jamshid" was the correct way to pronounce Jumpshit's name. In Persian mythology and folklore, Jamshid is described as the fourth and greatest king of the epigraphically unattested Pishdadian Dynasty (before the Kayanian dynasty). I'm glad I didn't try that hilarious remark when I met him on arrival.

Jamshid now holds a senior position in the government of Uzbekistan.

Lost in France

6. Weeping on hotel steps
France

"Our great weakness lies in giving up."
Thomas. A. Edison

Dear Brendan,

It wasn't until two years after retirement, that I realised that I needed to get physically fit or, at least, that I certainly should be a lot fitter. Rod, a long-time good friend of ours took me for a pint one day. He knew I was looking to raise money for the charity Operation Smile. Rod softened me up after a while and sprang the question.

"How about a bike ride?" he asked.

"Blimey, Rod, I haven't ridden a bike seriously for nearly forty years!" I gasped.

"Well, I'm doing it. Don't tell me you can't do what I can?" Rod was pretty much a chain smoker since a teenager. He knew about my missing lung and he was goading me.

I responded in kind. "Look, if you can do it, you wreck of a human being then it will be a piece of cake for me. Count me in. What are we talking about, ten miles, twenty…?" I had no idea what I had suddenly committed to.

"This year, you have a choice of a three-day or five-day ride. So it will be either two hundred and fifty or three hundred and eighty miles." I stared blankly into space.

He was in the selling groove and had started to assume he had made the sale.

"You'll need a proper road bike and, of course, serious training. Which means, mon ami, you'll probably have to do at least two fifty to three hundred miles in preparation to build stamina over the next two months. You'll room share with me don't worry. We have a support team that ensures we leave in the morning and arrive in the evening and they will be on standby for any unexpected events. We have route maps and there will be about two hundred riders." He had been talking fast to make sure I couldn't interrupt; however, I burst in at this stage.

"Unexpected events? Room share? Don't we go home at night? Two hundred and fifty miles? Training? What the hell are we talking about Rod?"

"Paris to Hayling Island, in July. We always make sure it's the week the French celebrate Bastille Day, so lots of fun. I'll register you so all you have to do is pay the cost. I'm doing the three-day ride which is only three hundred quid or so. Bloody bargain mate. I'll register you tonight." He had closed the deal in one fell swoop.

Fun? This didn't sound anything like fun.

A funny reason to weep

The ride started in Evreux about 70 miles from Paris. We were taken there by coach from Hayling Island via a ferry and our bikes travelled in a large lorry along with the small bags we were allowed - for overnight needs - and a change of cycling gear. It took about 10 hours to get to Paris. We stayed in La Defense, Paris and cycled 95 miles to Rouen the next day. On the third day, we cycled another 85 to Le Havre. It was harder than I first thought and I learned some new things about myself. For me, it was tough physically but that wasn't the toughest part. The mental demands were worse. I had no experience of a long physical effort over many hours and it can suddenly bring out emotions which we all keep under control fairly well in the course of a normal day. After about fifty miles my stamina would be very low. Then a hill might appear ahead. It could be one of two types of hill. First the short, very steep but straight hill. The other is the deceptive killer. The long, winding incline. Rarely, is there a combination. But the road we took from Paris to Rouen had a combination hill, about ten miles from the hotel in Rouen and rest. We took the best part of an hour to get up this four-mile hill! Rod was stronger than me but I had good bursts of energy but my lung capacity didn't supply enough oxygen to the blood; consequently, my legs would go wobbly and I had to get off the bike and pant heavily for about five minutes.

On our attempt to conquer this hill, about halfway up, I had to stop. I laid flat on the grass verge and waited for Rod.

He appeared, gradually getting closer. He saw me, pulled off beside me, took out a pack of Rothmans King Size, lit a ciggy, inhaled with enormous force and said, "Aaaaaaaahhhhhhhh, that's better!" I laughed hysterically for five minutes. A proper, real, side-splitting, belly laugh. Not something I had done since I was a child.

At the end of the third day, we finished our journey in Le Havre. I found it hard to stop. It was difficult to accept that it was over. I sat down on the steps outside the hotel and wept. Looking back, it sounds daft but, up to this point, I hadn't expected I would complete the ride.

We celebrated hard. I remember only two things about that evening. Firstly, Rod was making his way through a half-pint of Calvados when I went to bed and secondly when he arrived in our room, an hour or two later, he collapsed on his bed, fully clothed, on his back and passed out. I turned him over on his side. Rod had a very quiet ferry crossing the next morning to England.

As ever,

Paul

Note from author: The above was the first of fifteen charity rides I did. The most memorable of these I have described in a daily log included in a letter below. That ride was undertaken a month after Brendan passed away. Of all fifteen, this ride was the closest to having 'fun' and I still felt the need to write; to make him smile. I've added it to the letter I wrote originally.

Team C - all dressed up and 400 miles to go

Dear Brendan,

The ride is best described by a few facts and figures. However, I've provided a narrative instead.

Monday, 13th July — Ouistreham to Evreux: Day 1 Plan Miles, 90: Actual Miles, 97 (Urg!).

Set off at 06:30 am from the overnight ferry. Nothing open yet. No cafes, bars or other appropriate establishments selling vital hydration liquids. After 20 mins, Barrie (one eye, steel rod in his back and missing a thyroid - team nicknamed him "lucky") went over on loose gravel. Had cuts and bruises on his arm. He kept calling out for a nurse so we poured cold water over his arm and he continued under protest. Took until 8:00 am to open our account in a small bar and it appeared they had only opened by mistake and had completely forgotten it was a Monday. Suitably rehydrated we eventually left. Rained all morning. Got to the hotel in Evreux at 7:45 pm. Discovered that the hotel was the same as last year and did not provide soap, shampoo etc., or even more than one towel between two people without request (actually it was more begging than request). Only place to eat in town that would take us without a booking was something called 'The London Pub'. In France, this is not good. Hit the sack early clutching a half-used tub of Sudocrem. Woke up an hour later at 11:45 pm to a pre-Bastille Day firework display. Severe white flashing light followed by sounds that only the military are normally familiar with. Roommate continued to sleep and snored like a hurricane at the top of a mountain. He was at least washed and dried. When the fireworks stopped, I think I heard Barrie still calling for a nurse further down the corridor.

Tuesday 14th July — Evreux to Versailles, Paris: Day 2 Plan Miles, 60; Actual Miles, 65.

Bastille Day, as significant a public holiday as any in the French calendar. Had a lie-in. Started at 07:30 am after lovely breakfast of dishwasher coffee and a hard, crusty roll. Our route notes had warned us not to expect anything to be open between our hotel and Versailles, Paris. For once, our route notes were right. Rural France seems closed most of the time anyway, but on Bastille Day even tumbleweed has a day off. At around mid-day, we were getting desperate. As we struggled through a small farming community called Le Mesnil-Simon, Paul B spotted a flutter of flags hanging loosely outside a barn. The team waited while I went to investigate. As I went through, I met firemen, policemen, the village Maire (Mayor) and 200 villagers who had assembled, seated, along trestle tables. Food and drink were being brought out from the back of the barn. To cut a long story short, the Maire agreed that the '5 Desperados' could join the celebration for €15 a-head. It was to be an all-you-can-eat-and-drink five-course Bastille Day binge. We settled into the middle of the villagers. Although water was needed, only large glasses of red and rosé wine were given out. We started to make friends around us. Smatterings of French and English were swapped. Suddenly, a man in his early 70s appeared wearing a short jacket rather like a matador's. It was black and silky. His toupee was also black and silky. He picked up the microphone switched on his background music player and started out with his best impressions of Charles Aznavour, Sacha Distel and Maurice Chevalier. Unfortunately, it was more in the style of an Irish pub singer after 14 pints of Guinness. Looking back, it was just the warm-up artist that Barrie ("Lucky") needed.

Our new French singer's repertoire lasted as long as the five courses and multiple bottles of local vin. It was then time for the Maire to make his speech. It was obviously the annual "Haven't we done well," morale-boosting, "More turnips this year than any time in our history," rousing speech. Most of the villagers were well on their way to la-la land. Most of my team were too. It was a relief to all when he wrapped up. Then he turned to the team and welcomed us in French. Barrie could not resist his natural inclinations. He rose and swayed to the front to hug and kiss the Maire. Barrie's attention switched to the Maire's wife. He hugged and kissed her. She was to translate his English to French. Barrie is a Geordie (from Newcastle), his French is not good but he has the knack of finding a good word to use at the right moment even if it's not exactly correct. After the Maire welcomed us, Barrie took the microphone and began his response.

Barrie addresses the teeming mass in the barn

To describe Barrie's address to the teeming mass in the
barn as similar to the Henry V speech before the Battle of
Agincourt would be an exaggeration, but it isn't much of one.
After each sentence that he delivered, he kissed the wife of the
Maire. The whole barn cheered at each kiss. As he finished,
the villagers spontaneously rose as one to sing 'God Save The
Queen'. Barrie immediately responded by leading the
gathering in a rousing rendition of 'La Marseillaise'. It was
time to leave. It took us another 20 minutes to leave as the
Maire's wife offered us to stay the night. We could be put up
all around the village. I admit that the prospect seemed better
than a minimalist hotel with one towel between two but then
staying could involve pigs, goats and chickens or even worse
— that toothless stranger who kept coming in and out of the
barn door but didn't ever sit with the rest of the village. The
Maire gave one of us his email address so photos could be

swapped and about 40 of the villagers came out to look at our bikes and hug and kiss us all goodbye. My French is not that good but I'm sure we were invited back, same time, same place next year.

3 Hours later, still trying to leave

Back on the bikes, we noticed we had stayed more than 3 hours and had 35 miles still to go. Barrie started to call out for a nurse. Arrived in Versailles late, got to the hotel. Soap and shampoo available. Pizza was available. Slept like a stone. Roommate said I snored like a rhinoceros.

Wednesday 15th July — Paris to Rouen: Day 3 Plan Miles, 91: Actual Miles, 97 (gruelling but beautiful ride)/

Had more bother getting out of Paris in the rush hour (actually I think the rush hour is spread over 4 hours). As we got to the outskirts, we met the River Seine and essentially the route to Rouen follows this river. It was the most picturesque route of the week. One of the 'points-of-interest' (are there any when your backside is raw, your muscles are screaming and your head was under-hydrated the day before?) we passed was Monet's Garden at Giverny. Apparently, this is worth a visit. Fat chance. We arrived in Rouen after a four-mile gruelling uphill grind (after an 85-mile slog) in good time for a 10:30 pm mediocre meal. Rouen is where Joan of Arc was burned at the stake by the British at the age of 19 in 1431. Happy days. Towels on demand.

Thursday 16th July — Rouen to La Havre: Day 4 Plan Miles, 73 (fewer miles but bigger hills).

Frankly, this day was a blur. We recorded 39.5 degs Celsius on the bikes. We stopped frequently. I repeat, hydration is vital and we knew how to hydrate. Don't think anything was remarkable this day if you ignore fabulous French countryside. After arriving at the beach in Le Havre we checked-in to a minimalist hotel. Almost out of Sudocrem. Starting to panic. Roommate and I agreed that we probably didn't snore that night because neither of us heard the other one.

Friday 17th July — La Havre to Caen (& Ouistreham Ferry): Plan Miles, 80: Actual Miles, 80 — including journey home next day after the ferry. Tough hills today including a very scary bridge over the mouth of the River Seine as it flows into The English Channel (the French call it The Channel). It rained hard again and I was so cold I saw my breath panting out as I rode the highways and byways (what a contrast from yesterday's inferno). Highlight of the day was stopping at Pegasus Bridge near Caen and visiting Café Gondree which was the first house in France to be liberated, in 1944, following the D-Day landings. Madam Gondree, who was just six years old when this happened still owns and works behind the bar.

After rounds of rehydration, I noticed a large chap in short-legged red trousers and a light T-shirt hanging around in the bar. I called him over as he was on his own. He turned out to be a German called Max from Dresden. At this point, I have to point out that political correctness doesn't allow me to communicate all that was said, sung or discussed (in particular the subject of Bomber Harris and Dresden). "Mad Max," as we inevitably dubbed him, didn't explain why, of all the places to visit, he chose Café Gondree. Also, why he was so inadequately dressed for such a cold and damp day. We left Mad Max wondering what had happened to him. On the 8-mile journey to the hotel, I fell off my bike. Head, shoulder, arm, hand and leg contusions ensued. I called out for a nurse; Barrie made an unprintable remark.

We landed back in England on Saturday 18th July.

As ever,

Paul.

"Mad Max" with Barrie

PS: Below are some vignettes from these bike rides which I think might tickle your sense of humour and/or pathos. These are a few stories about characters I have met or have heard about over a pint.

Albert and Alf

These gentlemen were over 65; one was blind, the other deaf and they rode together on a tandem. As one of them said before we set out, "It took us about three minutes of a practice ride to agree who should go on the front and who should ride at the back." Three minutes? The keyword in that sentence was "agree." They squabbled endlessly about everything. To most people on the planet, it would be obvious who should go at the front. Given their relationship, it was consequently a real pleasure for anyone to be at a traffic light waiting to set off on green with Albert and Alf trying to co-ordinate when to go. As you may know, co-ordination when riding tandem is vital and setting off at lights has to be executed well. One could see, the other hear. Albert (front) was fond of talking, particularly to any ladies on the ride, so he paid no attention when bunched up with the ladies at traffic lights. Alf, whose use of the 'F' word was prodigious, shouted to his front-man to move but, of course, Albert couldn't hear. They eventually developed a series of code tapping on backs and arms to let the other one know, what was needed from the other. They then chose to act on, or ignore, the code. Sometime during the second day, I began to notice that at the way stops, lunch or dinner Albert and Alf sat apart, not talking to each other but trying to find someone else to chat to. I saw one older man sitting at the same lunch table as Albert looking very bemused as he chatted away. Albert was oblivious to the non-English responses he was getting. They were not the last ones to arrive at the end of the third and final day of cycling. I believe they came in about 15 minutes behind Rod and me. When they had completed their ride, they hugged each other and cried. Nobody knew for which charity they were riding.

Jed

Jed was in his mid-fifties. He was well known and well-liked. Over the period of the ride, I only ever saw him roaring drunk. He must have been a very good cyclist because he set off last, cycled alone and arrived at the final destination of the day among the early arrivals. I saw him drinking a bottle of red wine at breakfast, lunch, the mid-afternoon way stop and, when I arrived at the final stop of the day, he was there again with a bottle. I saw him on the planned route on two occasions. Once, he was swigging from a red wine bottle whilst actually cycling and another when he was passed out on the side of the road in the middle of the most beautiful French countryside. We called a support team member to come and check on him, for ticks if nothing else.

Jed was riding for Breast Cancer. His wife had died five weeks before the ride.

Derek

Derek's wife insisted that he only go on the ride if he was constantly with a small team, never alone, day and night, and his teammates would keep an eye on him. He had never ridden a bike before but had done more training than the average rider in preparation.

In Paris, things went well for the first twenty minutes as Derek and his teammates set off from their hotel in Paris for the long ninety-two-mile day to Rouen. Derek however, needed a pee just as they were going around the Arc de Triomphe and he shouted out to his team he was "Just popping into the nearest pissoir." Unfortunately, no one heard him as he swerved off the road to the open-air ironwork standing on the pavement as the rest of the team pounded their pedals towards Rouen. Two or three minutes later he came out of the ironwork pissoir just in time to see a cyclist disappear along a street roughly in the direction poor old Derek thought he should go. By chance, it wasn't one of the Paris to Hayling Bike Ride participants and he headed in the wrong direction. A few minutes later, the other team members backtracked to try and find Derek and came to the last place they remember him being with them. After some diligence and a lot of side-street searching they gave up, called the support team to report he'd gone missing and went on their way to Rouen.

After six hours of driving around the most likely routes Derek could have taken, he was not to be found. The support team reported Derek missing to the nonplussed Gendarmerie. After two days, Derek was arrested in a barn loft of a farm near the German border. He was in a state of exhaustion, and was hungry, scared and aggressive. The farmer had reported hearing an intruder in his barn to the local police. When they turned up, Derek started to fight with them as he didn't speak French and couldn't work out why they didn't speak English. When the support team arrived to pick him up, they had enough information to placate the police. Derek's wife finally confessed to the support team, when confronted with the situation, the reason he was on the ride. He was suffering from early Alzheimer's. After several hours, they released Derek on the condition that he was sent home immediately. New rules were made about riders having diagnosed dementia. Unfortunately, new 'gallows humour' jokes were made up by the rest of the exhausted, hungry and aggressive riders.

Jim

It was a wet evening and the small group of male cyclists were making their way back to their hotel in Paris after a hearty pasta meal. Pasta is an ideal food for cycling endurance. A small corner bar was attractively lit and beckoned them in for a nightcap. Jim and the others were really tired but wide awake. In they went. There were the usual Parisian style suspects smoking, drinking and talking at or around the bar area. Jim and his mates started on beer ("for hydration purposes") and migrated downwards rapidly to Pastis, Pernod or cognac. They used their limited French to engage the locals. Jim, a quiet, unassuming, slightly boring purchasing manager slowly latched on to a dark-haired, voluptuous lady who clearly had taken a fancy to this English gentleman. Music came on the juke-box, something typically French and romantic. Several people started to dance including Jim and his new friend. They danced close at the slow numbers and fast at the quicker tempo. More drinking, more dancing. Jim's mates tired more quickly than him. Astonished and ready for bed, they all said goodnight to Jim with his room share asking him not to wake him up when he came in. This was not to be a problem.

Jim's room share woke with the alarm clock chiming away. Jim was not there. As the cyclists emerged from their sleep pits brightly clad in lycra, spandex, figure hugging socks and sturdy headgear each one grabbed their route notes for the day, filled their water bottles, grabbed a banana to tuck into their shirt pocket and off they went, grunting, wheezing, swearing and singing. Most times they started with "The Long and

Winding Road" but later, group singing disintegrated into small teams of blues, negro spirituals and the 'Blaydon Races' (for some obscure reason). Personally, I like a good old sing-song, but not when I'm out of breath!

Jim's bike was the only one left in the underground car park. Support members called Jim's room share mobile phone and were told he didn't come home and "I'm not his bloody keeper!" Retracing Jim's whereabouts was easy up to the point where he left the bar with the dark-haired lady whom nobody appeared to know or had seen before or knew where she lived or even her name. Oh dear.

Jim actually didn't ever reappear that week. No one knew what had happened or what transpired that evening, after the bar. The leader of the bike ride was left to explain to Jim's wife and family at the ferry port as we arrived back. Police had been informed and so had the British Embassy in Paris. No one knew what to say or what to do next.

Nothing was known for quite a while. Then word got out that Jim had joined a caravan of gypsies in Paris, had gone with them to the Camargue, in the south of France, where they have a camp. Apparently, he married the dark, mysterious woman from the bar in a gypsy wedding (bigamy, not a problem apparently) and decided that managing purchasing for a small company wasn't going to be his thing for the rest of his life. We all felt unbelievably sad for his family. You couldn't make it up.

Epilogue

There are many stories of course, but I'll stop now. The number of people alone who were cycling, over a five-day period, during the fifteen years I participated in the ride would determine that there would be a few anecdotes. Personal tragedy, an odd couple, strange disappearances or acts of kindness at the very least it seems.

There have been heart attacks and broken bones. People have completed rides blind, deaf, with one leg, wired jaw, in need of a hip replacement, broken nose and cheek-bone... and many other disabilities which would put fewer hardy people off. Each rider raises money for a charity of their choice. We have had nurses, doctors, accountants, a homeless man and his son, a high court judge, a fading rock star, recovering alcoholics, recovering lawyers, tree surgeons, professional boxers (six in one team), etc. The oldest rider (so far) was eighty; the youngest, fourteen. I thought I was raising the age limit until I met seventy-four-year-old Ron, a retired farmer with bow legs.

Inevitably, there are true heroes. I am now riding each year with a team of five fellows and we look after one another. Each of them has had a tragedy in their lives which inspired them to raise money for others.

My old chum Rod is part of the support team and I room share with him each year. However, I've never seen him drink Calvados again.

As ever,
Paul

7. "So what do you want to be when you grow up?" Kuwait

Dear Brendan,

I'm going to call him Sean to protect his modesty, although that is entirely the wrong word.

Sean was an American and spoke with a strong southern accent. I believe he had operated as a riverboat gambler after leaving school. He was a chain smoker, outrageous drinker and the smartest person I'd ever worked with. Highly analytical, articulate and hard-working, customers loved him (mostly). He always introduced himself to customers as "A shy, sweet and innocent Southern boy." Sean retired in 2002. This is all relevant to the situation in which I found myself in 2004, a year after I had retired.

Despite my resolve to change my life completely when I retired, I accepted an invitation from Tamim, a former colleague, to run a five-day project with the board of a bank in the Middle East. I have always liked to visit somewhere new and that sounded interesting "...and after all," I said to Angela. "It's only for five days."

The project needed two of us so Sean and I signed up and arrived in Kuwait after supplying the bank with the five-day plan. The bank is no slouch of a bank. The issues they wanted to discuss and agree action were about competition and technological innovation.

Sean first became tetchy on arrival when, to his horror, we were made aware that alcohol was illegal in Kuwait. Not just frowned upon or severely limited, but illegal. We were told by both our sponsors and the bank that under no circumstances were we to obtain or even ask for alcoholic beverages. We then realised just how long five days were going to be.

Our routine for interviews meant alternating between us - who asked the questions and who documented the responses. We agreed that I would ask the questions of senior members. Then we would switch, with Sean taking the juniors and me taking the notes.

The CEO of the bank was the first interviewee. We were there at his request and therefore it was essential he set the tone for our visit. He immediately told us that he was Palestinian, made homeless by Israel twice and then thrown out of his own country. He arrived in Kuwait and joined a bank in 1961. He was made CEO in 1983 but fled Kuwait to save his life in 1990 when Saddam Hussein's Iraq invaded. He told us Saddam hated Palestinians more than anyone else. From reports, Saddam indeed butchered Palestinians more than most when he occupied the country. The interview with the CEO was difficult. He steadfastly avoided giving any information on the subjects he wanted us to tackle. He almost didn't blink when looking straight at me for most of the hour we spent in his VERY expensively furnished office. He didn't want to discuss details of the issues, he just encouraged us to get the answers from the executive workshop in three days. He wanted us to feel the enormity of his presence and power in Kuwait. He was one of the country's most famous people, after the Kuwait

Royal Family. Sean and I agreed after the meeting that the whole short project was a test of his board members and executives. We were just facilitating the CEO's appraisal of them. At that time in Kuwait, competitive and technological banking issues were pretty straight forward choices to solve.

All our other interviews were well-organised with briefings beforehand and de-briefings post-interview. The interviewees all wore the formal Dishdasha. Sean was beginning to snarl at the end of the first (sober) day. The second day of interviews began with a sombre briefing about the Treasurer we were about to meet. Apparently, his father had died ten days previously and it was suggested that we were to be sensitive and passive in our interview. I took the lead on this one, as previously agreed and for obvious reasons (Sean's mood). The interview went really well, we got all the information we needed and more. He was very friendly, laughed a lot, cracked a few jokes and talked about being a Manchester United fan. Sean and I agreed at the end that he appeared in very good spirits. When our de-briefing began, I started by saying that for someone whose father had recently passed he appeared a very happy and relaxed man.

"Yes, well I suppose so," said our minder. "He did inherit $1.3 billion from his father."

We sat in silence for at least ten seconds and then I said, "But why would he still be working as Treasurer in the bank if he has all this money?"

"Well, he already had $400 million of his own money, plus houses in London, California and the far east. Not ignoring the several $350,000 cars and boats. He likes to work here; it is a real challenge for him. He'd be bored otherwise. He's the first one in the bank every morning."

Although the rest of the interviews were factual and passed without incident worth recalling, it was obviously the 'social environment' of our long, dry evenings that was getting to Sean. He is a hard person to ignore when he smells blood and several executives were not passing (his) muster. Vague or ineffectual answers were greeted with audible snorts of disdain from our fearless, ex-riverboat gambler. I had seen him grumpy before but this was on a new level.

The big day arrived. We greeted all the attendees to our workshop and waited for the CEO. He came in, sat down and stared at me. I kicked off with the day's structure, purpose, agenda and timings.

Sean was to open with an analysis of the global and Middle East marketplace for Financial Services and banking. It was to be a standard 'strengths, weaknesses, opportunities and threats industry analysis' which we had researched and structured into a punchy 'so you had better do something' twenty-minute, one-way presentation. I'd seen him do this many times in different situations and he was particularly strong and loud on this occasion; I didn't need to wonder why. The enforced sobriety wasn't going well. At the conclusion, Sean looked straight at the CEO, paused and said,

"Every time I meet a new CEO, I always ask them the same question. So, what do you want to be when you grow up?" Sean was looking directly and unflinchingly at the CEO.[5]

The CEO stared at Sean and then turned and stared at me. Every one of the bank's executives visibly shrank in their

---

[5] This type of situation had happened twice before with Sean in Belfast but, most stressfully, at the TUC Conference in Watford in 1997 to which we were invited to brief the heads of unions about the impact of technology (computers) on low skilled employees (now there's a poison chalice!)

seats and froze. Me? Let's just say it was a very difficult moment. Do I jump in as I used to, before my retirement, in awkward moments with customers to divert attention and relieve tension?

Instinct told me to hold back this time.

After the proverbial 10 seconds, which seemed like 10 hours, the CEO flung his head back and burst out laughing. The executives were still frozen in their seats. I wondered whether laughter was a good or bad sign. The CEO stood up and pointed at Sean who had not moved a muscle. He was staring back at the big boss who then said in a very loud voice, "I like you! Please treat everyone as badly as this for the rest of the day and I will come back for a summary of the results."

He left the room, but the executives were as taut as piano wire for the whole day. The atmosphere in the workshop was less than creative. When we concluded, the CEO returned to grunt, scowl and redirect the conclusions to what was obviously his planned outcome. We ended the workshop and the CEO requested for both of us to come to his office for a debrief. This was going to be entirely about our assessment of the individuals on the executive committee. He asked the same question of us about each of his people. "Should I fire him?" Sean and I had agreed that I would field any questions that might arise concerning the CEO's executives. I had had some experience of these type of questions before and I had found the best way to answer was to say, "Well for his role in the bank, we have learned that a person needs these skills and experiences..." and then go on to describe each role in this way...

"Unfortunately, as we have no extended experience of working with him, I cannot assess with great conviction whether he possesses some or all of what is needed. You would be the best one to judge that."

His laugh filled the room and the connecting corridors for the second time that day. He dismissed us. It was the first time I had felt like executive jewellery.

A simple request

Sean and I caught the last BA flight out that day to London. It was an oasis. Luckily, we sat in different parts of business class. In those days, passengers were served whatever drink they asked for before take-off. I heard Sean placed a sizeable order to the sympathetic BA cabin staff and I knew all was right in his world again. Next to me sat an Arab gentleman who ordered eleven whisky miniatures before take-off and when the BA cabin crew said they couldn't serve him any more before take-off, he started on the bagged bottle of duty-free he had tucked away by his feet. Alcohol is permitted to be exported from Kuwait. He was very drunk, very quickly and started to talk to me in a heavy Arabic accent, of which I understood less than ten per cent. After a while, it became obvious he was asking me questions, so I decided just to say why I was in Kuwait and which bank I had visited. Eventually, it turned out he was the cousin of the treasurer we had interviewed. He also mumbled that he hoped that I had been taken care of properly with my 'beverage needs'. I gave a puzzled look. Recognising my confusion, he explained that the Defence Minister was responsible for all 'beverage' handling in the country, and as foreigners, a simple request through his cousin would have stocked our hotel rooms.

I chose never to tell Sean.

I had never been happier to leave a situation.

Angela greeted me at home with, "Oh hi, you're back

already. That went quickly. Did you have a good trip?"

As ever,
Paul

PS: This is the last time I worked with Sean, although we have met several times since. Beverages were involved. He is a strong supporter of my charity fundraising and is currently a permanent member of 'Bubba's Bait, Tackle, Worms and Beer Bar,' Virginia Beach, Virginia, USA.

PPS: The CEO is still the head of the bank and all its subsidiaries (Author: at the time of writing).

PPPS: The local office (our sponsors for this trip) received several large orders for technology from the bank which they would not normally have expected to get. They said they didn't know why they had been so successful in that following year. As no one from the local office had attended the meeting there was nothing to connect our five days with the process of traditional selling.

There are several morals to this story.

Medieval castle of Torrechiara, Parma. Something I missed.

8. The Formula 1 Driver
Parma, Italy

Dear Brendan,

In February 1998, I made a pledge never to fly Alitalia again. I was requested to support a big campaign for a sales breakthrough with the largest pasta maker in Italy. The company was rapidly recruiting externally from all the well-known competitors. As it turned out, my knowledge of how to get things done 'inside the tent' was very useful to our new recruits.

I was in two minds when Michele Marcolini asked me to join his small team in a highly competitive bid at a customer's headquarters in Parma, Italy. Michele had been an early and very senior recruit from a competitor and he was my mentor for my next promotion. I always thought that the big splash bids he was talking about were a waste of time and resources. The kind of work we were bidding for in this part of the food chain was won on relationships and track record. In this case we had neither, except for the relationship with the IT Director. That relationship usually counted for nothing given the decision-makers and projects were upstream of any technology solutions we were normally involved in. So given this huge and obvious incompatibility, as quick as a flash, I said yes (Did I mention that Michele was my mentor for my next promotion?).

Angie encouraged me to go on the earliest flight from London to Milan so I could have a rare opportunity of free time. I would be able to see the historic and beautiful city of Parma or perhaps the medieval castle of Torrechiara before meeting Michele later in the evening. First flight was 6:45 am with Alitalia which meant getting up at 4:00 am on a bleak February morning. The flight was delayed, then cancelled and by two o'clock in the afternoon, I had been rescheduled to a three o'clock Alitalia flight arriving in Milan at six o'clock losing an hour for time zone differences. This had given me plenty of time to cancel my rental car, call Michele and explain the new timings and most importantly, check emails, make phone calls and review what I was to do as part of the team. In other words, it was a normal business trip with no free time. Michele would pick me up and drive me to Parma. Urgh!

Michele, a brilliant thinker and relationship builder with

clients, is not well-organised. He was late and drove me to his office building so he could "Do some last-minute things." We left there at 8:00 pm and drove to Parma along the E35 motorway at 300mph (well it bloody well seemed like it). We arrived at around 10:00 pm with me having had very little to eat or drink. I wondered what Parma was like. We had a briefing at dinner, which was mainly heaps of fruit, in the hotel with the small team of four. My stomach gurgled all night.

The next morning, we were met at the pasta company's headquarters by not one but two charming young Italian women. It was a typical head office on a manufacturing site; clean, tidy and functional and hugely lacking in character. As we were shown into the executive and then boardroom area it became more like a Swiss bank; oak-panelled, expensive ambient lighting with deep piled carpets. I suspected that it would be a rare occasion that factory workers and/or union officials would tread these corridors.

We were escorted to the boardroom where we were met by Paolo. He was charming and suntanned (in February?). His position was Finance Director and was one of the heirs to this pasta empire. A €5B revenue company operating in nine countries with 8,000 employees, Paolo and his two brothers owned 51%. Also, Paolo was previously a Formula 1 racing driver having retired eight years before. He was a smooth operator and sharp as a tack.

Before we started, we went through a side-door which led to a product display room and we each were asked to choose a product to take home with us. Not knowing much about pasta, I chose a product called 'Gemma', a specialist pasta. Our daughter Gemma was still at university and would appreciate dishing it out to her roommates.

After the morning session, we were invited into a very formal dining room next to the boardroom. It had photographs of Paolo driving his racing car in one of the Grand Prix races with other classic portraits of his father, mother and brothers. Paolo asked me to sit next to him and we chatted about English football, growing figs on the south coast of England and sport in general. Cricket didn't come up as a subject. I fished to see if he wanted to talk about racing cars but he didn't take the bait. I concluded he probably was sick to death of the subject so I dropped the idea. I let Michele know that I wanted him to slip in and establish a rapport with Paolo as I knew that if he liked me and we won any business here I'd have to be the contact and delivery executive. It's the nature of the work. It was part of our strategy for Michele to pick up this role but Paolo didn't want to play our game. He was sticking with me.

Lunch was unbelievably good but about five times as much food as I was used to in those days and I'd hardly eaten the day before, just heaps of fruit. The delightful but heavy pasta hit the pit of my stomach in a vaguely familiar way. Lunch finished and we left the executive dining room. Paolo announced that before we continued with the afternoon session we have a walking tour of the factory. Urgh!

I think in the previous ten years of customer work I must have made more factory visits than Queen Elizabeth II. We were on the factory floor when it happened. That indefinable feeling deep in your gut, together with a voice in your head which screams silently, "Get to a toilet NOW!"

I smiled at Paolo, the suave, sophisticated, suntanned and famous Italian ex-Formula 1 racing driver and asked, no I half-shouted, "I need to visit the toilet. Please tell me where the nearest is." He pointed to a door on the factory floor and said,

"That is the nearest, but you should go back to the boardroom where it is more civilised."

Without time to explain, I just put my head down and fled to the nearest. At that moment, being somewhere 'more civilised' was irrelevant. As I went through the door, I told them not to wait for me and I'd catch them up. Luckily, I didn't look at Michele.

As I entered through the 'mens' door, I quickly assessed my situation. There were holes in the floor with no screening between them. In fact, it was just one room with rows of holes in the floor, footmarks as guides and washbasins attached to the walls. I was in my best business clothes; dark blue suit, white shirt, red tie. Knowing what was likely to happen, I urgently removed all my lower garments, shoes and socks whilst the few factory workers in the room smiled. I'm definitely going to spare you anymore narrative about this situation. Imagination is enough, probably I have overshared already.

I found my way back to the boardroom where they were all waiting for me. Paolo had a twinkle in his eye. He smiled, a beaming, knowing smile. The other attendees had no idea what had transpired. I was next to talk about our experience in running transformation projects. I was 'going commando' (no underwear) at this point. My delivery was crisp, short and punchy.

Michele drove me back to Milan airport, again at 300 mph. Perhaps he had been inspired by the ex-racing driver; more likely it was just the way he and most of Italy drive. He was very grateful for my participation and said to me, "By the way, thanks! What a brilliant move for you to disappear during the factory tour. I liked the way you invented an excuse to let me take over with Paolo and I think he did too. He was smiling a lot. I was able to have a really good conversation and I believe he was impressed with me and how we worked as a team. I've realised people at our company are so inventive."

I left Michele at the airport terminal and he sped off. I noticed a huge crowd of people at the Alitalia check-in desk. The airline had cancelled the previous flight and were doing their very best to be vague, illusive, pouty with a smattering of shrugs and hand gestures. They were not issuing boarding passes with seat numbers. I already had a boarding pass and a seat number and felt this may work in my favour. I was assured by the Italian, state-owned and run Alitalia staff that this meant nothing.

"Why?" I begged. Always a mistake to beg to an Italian government employee. It trigged a smugness, not introduced before, into the conversation. "Because we are not sure if we can get everyone on the plane." She wanted to add, "You idiot" at the end of her sentence, but she didn't have to. The tilt of her head and a full pout was enough.

Here I was: a commando-attired executive in need of some quick thinking. The only flight back to London was this last Alitalia plane and I was wondering how many other people had realised that passengers for two flights would not fit into one plane. I sized up the landscape… which gate? Would there be a bus trip out to the plane? Where should I stand to get maximum elbow purchase in a swelling crowd? I positioned myself well enough to get through the Alitalia staff passport and boarding pass checkpoint. The people getting on the first two buses had worked all these logistical dynamics out way ahead of the easy-going, talkative, disorganised, infrequent flyers. I was on the second bus. As I stood on the tarmac waiting to climb the mobile stair ramp to the plane door it started to rain. Gently at first, then as I stepped through the door into the plane it poured. I looked at the seat I had assigned and saw someone was sitting there. I quickly realised it was a grab-any-seat-sit-down-and-occupy occasion. I grabbed a window seat about four rows back from the door. The rest of the plane filled up. Not a seat to be had. I looked out of the window to see about ten people still standing on the mobile steps. Then I saw another bus approaching. It emptied all the occupants, closed the doors and drove back to the terminal leaving about sixty to seventy people standing in the rain. Some were on the stairs but barred from entering the plane, and the rest bunched around the bottom. The cabin crew started to gently and charmingly encourage those that were standing in the doorway to move back and explained that they would be helped when they were back in the terminal. Realising this was their last chance to board, two or three of them pushed forward. The door was closed with what must have been very strong Italian swear words shouted and I heard one or two familiar English expletives coming from further down the stairwell. As the plane pushed back, I saw the unlucky, abandoned and soaking wet Alitalia passengers standing, some still optimistically, on the mobile stair, alone on a dark, cold, puddled, February tarmac watching in disbelief. No bus in sight. As we took off, I could see all of them trudging back on the long path to the terminal in the driving rain. I'm sure there were aviation, health and safety and human rights laws broken several hundred times.

Arriving home very late, Angie asked me, "How was historic Parma?"

"I'm not ready to tell you," I said.

As ever,

Paul

PS: I will never fly Alitalia again.

PPS: We won the pasta company's business from the incumbent, arch competitors.

PPS: Michele turned out to be a big hero for our Italian business.

PPPS: I didn't support any campaigns in Italy again, but I did get promoted.

PPPPS: I've never been back to Parma and never eaten that particular company's pasta.

PPPPPS: It's funny how a dicky tummy can bear fruit.

There will be something waiting in the long grass

9. The Long Grass
Belfast

Dear Brendan,

I had heard the Irish expression, "I'll catch you in the long grass" before. It meant someone was going to get you sometime, somehow, sooner or later and you won't see it coming. I experienced its meaning in Belfast.

By 1995, I had been lucky enough to have worked and lived in many countries but I had never set foot in Northern Ireland. Then, suddenly, I spent a year there, on and off.

A huge part of the challenge of building a new business inside an established Corporation was fending off the established ways of doing business. It was made clear by the new CEO that the company would go to market with a new approach, bringing new services closely tailored to our customers business needs. It sounded blindingly obvious.

By 1995, the sales force was beginning to understand how different the work my teams did was from 'normal' stuff. Most of them were selling hammers and nails and didn't much like it if the solution needed glue, needle and thread or joinery. They had felt threatened, but through working together in market planning, we were getting some significant breakthroughs. Having been an account manager previously, I knew that to be included in the account planning process with the account team or leader was essential. With one such account, a well-known bank, we arrived at a plan to break the grip of our arch competitors. Our work should payback for the whole company food chain if successful.

Belfast

I got the call to bid for work, based in Belfast. They had put to tender a project to, "Improve the performance of our Branch Network." There had been an incumbent competitor for this type of work for several years and I'm pretty sure our account leader only asked for my team to be added so he could learn how we put together a response for such a project and, well, if we win, he gets a bonus!

I had recruited Sean (you may remember him from my Kuwait letter a couple of weeks ago) to our team some months before and I asked him and another colleague to help put the proposal together. We stayed in the Europa Hotel, Belfast the night before our sales presentation. The Europa was known at the time as the 'most bombed hotel in Europe' and also the 'most bombed hotel in the world' after having suffered 28 bomb attacks during the troubles. A detail I had not let slip to Angie.

Four other companies, including the prestigious and incumbent firm, were bidding; I had asked to be last. We knocked them dead and won the work. After the usual celebrations and chest-puffing, I then thought, "Dear God, we now have to deliver."

One of the many things I had not appreciated about Northern Ireland was the huge Scottish ancestry and its cultural influence on institutions such as banks. The CEO, who loved our presentation, was Daire; the Operations Director, David, and Projects Director, Andrew. Andrew was to be our minder.

The bank was one of the three largest in Ireland, north and south. It had more branches in the Republic than in Northern Ireland (NI). They had the complicated arrangement of NI being the main decision-maker at that time as it was wholly owned by a major UK bank. Our project had been narrowed to review the branch network in the north only. Our goal was described to us: "To radically re-engineer the branch network in NI." I was to find out later that one man's "radical" was another man's "incremental" but, as it turned out, radical was needed, badly.

Our team, supplemented by bank employees set about our task in a structured, fact-based, data-gathering exercise in a sample set of branches. I had appointed Jon as project leader; Sean was to be the main analyst. I went off elsewhere to sell more work, prepare more proposals and review other current projects underway, in several customers.

I called Jon and Sean, regularly. Jon was happy because the project plan was being executed according to schedule and budget with no issues arising in project execution. However, I was more concerned with Sean. Being a truly lapsed Catholic, most of his dealings with the "proddies" (as he referred to them) were obviously conducted with a hair shirt under his shamrock tie. Keep this in mind. He kept telling me that he'd never been into a bank quite like this. Each branch did things uniquely.

"OK, well, give me examples Sean."

"OK, well let's take current account statements. We've found a town branch in the Ballymena district who on a Friday regularly call their customers. Only some of them live in the town, those who don't are asked if there is any shopping to be done…"

He paused for my inevitable next question but then continued before I could speak. He was toying with me and I knew it.

"…they pop into the shops on their way to hand-delivering their statements." He waited.

"They print? Hand deliver? Shop?"

Statement printing was a non-standard practice in banking in 1995 in most of the UK. Delivering by hand was unheard of.

"Well, actually, only to some customers. Those they don't know personally have to wait until the postman comes on Saturday."

"And the shopping?"

"Well," he hesitated to get more impact. "Some older or infirm people can't get out as much as they used to, so as the bank hand-deliver their statement it seemed a good idea (it was of course, but good business performance? No) to ask if there is any shopping they want… and if they'd like some cash brought along. Most of the customers withdraw just the amount of cash they'll need for the next week so there really isn't much activity shown on the account statement anyway. The branch in the next village expects their customers to come into the branch, no matter who they are, to pick up a statement if they want one. That branch wasn't too bothered either way." He gave other examples for the next 30 minutes and then I let him get back to his bottle of 'redders'.

The room for improvement was enormous and what we were finding all over the branch network was a huge gulf between best practice and reality. The challenge was to show how it could be done. The interesting cultural customer delivery service was definitely a wonderful social benefit to have… but affordable?

We prepared our final report and decided to test it on the Regional Manager, Northern Ireland, at his monthly branch managers meeting before reviewing with the Daire's executive team. All the branch managers and senior regional staff of NI were to be there. Sean and I waited to go in. The door opened and we entered. It was like walking into an open grave. All the usual tried and tested ways of breaking the ice were met with stony silence. Everyone in the room, except Sean and me, were hardcore male Northern Irelanders, over fifty-five with a stoic, grey and ashen stare. We showed an enormous opportunity for branch efficiency improvements and a practical plan for the implementation of that improvement.

Silence. No one even coughed.

I asked for feedback. The Regional Manager asked me

what we "…intended to do with this fecking shite?"

Because of the way I think and react under extreme pressure, my sense of humour wanted to ask why he was using curse words from what I had always thought were from the Republican side of the border. However, I didn't. I'm not that stupid.

I told the room that it was our plan to present this (fecking shite) to Daire's executive meeting at which the Regional Manager would be attending. Also in attendance, would be John M, the head of the bank in the Republic of Ireland and John D, from the parent bank headquarters in London.

Silence. Hmmm, time to leave I thought.

I thanked everyone for their time and that of their staff. The friendliness and helpfulness of their staff in the branch network made our job so much easier I said. Sean and I headed for the door. Just as we thought we were free, a menacing voice came from behind us.

"I will catch you in the long grass. Make no mistake." There was a slight Scottish lilt to his hard Ulster accent.

Daire, the CEO, was a professorial, enthusiastic and pleasant man. He had one eye which appeared considerably larger than the other and which rarely blinked. Rumour had it that he shopped for his clothes in Oxfam and only bought discounted perishable food on a Friday when the 'best before' food was about to be binned. I could see why the rumour persisted. He was very thin, slight and smelt of mothballs.

I had the good sense to walk through everything with him, the Operations Director (David) and the Projects Director (Andrew) before the meeting and agreed some very minor, cosmetic changes to the report. Daire was excited but David and Andrew, I suspected, had been in the long grass once or twice before.

We delivered the report to the formal meeting. It was accepted entirely and we won the follow-on work to help implement the changes. I tried not to think what lay in the long grass or in fact just where the long grass might be. My guess was it could be anywhere, at any time and would involve a memorable event.

On the journey home, I found myself sitting next to the Reverend Dr Ian Paisley on the flight from Belfast to London. The plane had been delayed 30 mins with no explanation. I was in row 1 seat A. He came in the aircraft, the doors closed and he took up row 1, seats B and C. As you may know, he was a large man and at that moment he was more than slightly out of breath and sweating like a Turkish wrestler. I froze. I sat beside him overwhelmed. He said nothing but was served by the cabin crew. Scottish Whiskey if I remember correctly.

"Is he English?"

As a team, we had made a favourable impression on our first project. One-off projects would not sustain a business as ambitious and driven as our group was in those days, so the next step was to build a working relationship with Daire, CEO. I proposed four additional projects to the follow-on to Branch Performance Improvement project. He bought all four. The previous competitive firm was asked to bid but failed. Price wasn't the reason, surprisingly; Daire didn't like to be "colonised" as he put it! That was a 'note to file' for me to reflect on later.

A week before the four new projects started, he asked me to run through the teams and particularly the team leaders I intended to appoint. Towards the end, he asked, "Er, Rohini

Pinheiro, er, is he English?"

"Yes"

"Er, where was he born?"

"West London I believe, he is one of our brightest leaders."

"Er, what kind of name is this he has?"

"I believe his parents are of Sri Lankan origin."

"Ah, ok. Well, do you have another leader for this team?"

I paused. "I do have another leader, but Rohini is one of my best leaders and I have made him free of any other commitments in order to lead this team as I know how important..." Daire interrupted me by holding his hand inches from my face.

"Is the other leader English, born in England and of English parents?"

"Yes."

"OK, well, let's swap out Rohini on this one, for your other leader please."

"Of course, it is still possible to do that Daire, but honestly, I'm giving you our best available person for this particular job of product profitability..."

"Done, then. I expect the other leader here next week with your teams. Thank you, see you then." I left his office, absolutely seething and feeling torn and inadequate. Bugger. I didn't ever tell Rohini about the content of the discussion. He still doesn't know. Lions 1 Christians 0.

The following week, I received a phone call from Daire. "Paul, your new leader for the profitability project..."

I knew what he was going to say. "...she's a woman!"

"I'm sorry, Daire, I don't understand," I lied.

"You've appointed a woman as the project leader?" He

was getting agitated and I could visualise his larger eye getting larger.

"Er, yes Daire. I'm sorry you've lost me a bit on this one. Have you read her CV? Have you seen how much experience she has had in retail banking product profitability and with all the major leading retail banks?"

"Yes, but you should know that we tried a woman once in an important role and it didn't work out here."

"Well, here is the offer, Daire. If Janet does not deliver the project as defined and scoped, you don't pay us." I was maybe sticking my neck out a bit (actually a lot), but I was confident and it was an offer a man who shops in Oxfam for his clothes couldn't resist. I heard a muffled "Fuck!" but he agreed and put the phone down. Lions 1 Christians 1.

As expected, Janet delivered a superb project and her extraordinary performance as leader probably had nothing to do with what I had told her about a certain phone call.

During one of the key meetings of this project to which I had attended, one of our team, Marlo, gave an outstanding analysis of banking product profitability across Ireland, UK, Europe and North America. Daire asked Marlo and me to stay after the meeting to "Have a chat." Daire was clearly taken with Marlo. Towards the end of the "chat" and as he and I were leaving, Daire turned to Marlo and asked, "You have interesting experiences in other banks, Marlo, where were you born?" Oh dear, not again.

Marlo, a frank and emotional person replied, "I was born in Paris. My mother is Moroccan, my father Palestinian and we are Jewish. Two of my grandparents were Italian. Quite a combination, don't you think?" he said proudly. I was quite proud of him too. As we walked out of the CEO's office, I just could not bring myself to look at Daire's large eye.

Just burning money

One of the new projects had been cash management. A complicated subject at the best of times and it can have a significantly negative impact on a retail bank if done poorly. One of the interesting aspects of working in this bank was the fact that, as you may know, Northern Ireland prints its own banknotes in the same way as Scotland does. More specifically, a few selected banks print the money and this bank was one of those licensed by the Bank of England to do so. This not only entails printing but also destroying banknotes, through a custom-built furnace on the site of one of the bank's buildings. It happened every week and strict rules and processes were followed to ensure nothing went missing before the furnace!

I was invited to join the party one week. One senior executive, one operations' executive and one cash management senior manager had to be present at a minimum. I had two reasons to be there. Firstly, it sounded like a unique experience, and it was. Secondly, I had picked up that a lot of grapevine information was exchanged at these weekly meetings and, also, decisions were taken. When I looked at the book that recorded attendees each week, I saw that at least three or four other executives from various parts of the bank had turned up. The day I went, a privilege as I'm sure you can appreciate, my NI Regional Manager friend, he of the long grass, was there. Burning cash must have a special effect on mankind. We stood around while the most junior attendee did the work and the room took the ambience of pagan worship. It was hot and smelt as if Lucifer's beard had been singed. I picked up a few useful tips about how we could win further work and how some of our projects could turn into good traditional technology projects. As I left the room the NI Regional Manager walked beside me and said, "I haven't forgotten you. I came along to remind myself of what you looked like."

"Well, it was nice to see you also," I said, not meaning it.

Full and frank discussions

Our projects were coming to an end after almost a year and the traditional technology business was linking neatly into the picture. I proposed to Daire an executive workshop, offsite and two days in duration and he readily agreed as one of the benefits was to have a common focus on issues and accountable plans (I had projects in my mind) to resolve them. He chose a shabby hotel in Kildare on the edge of the Bog of Allen, in the Republic. It went well for one and a half days. The executive team had had full, frank and open discussions around some very tricky issues and had defined plans with allocated ownership to get them done. Apparently, this was unheard of in this bank. I felt really good. The last issue to be discussed was cash management. I asked Sean to come into the meeting as he had taken the lead on this project. Daire loved Sean. He knew (some) of his background and was particularly interested in the cash management projects he had run in the casinos of Macau, China. That was obviously before I had recruited him into our London based business. At the time Sean had worked there, gambling in Macau was expanding very rapidly and they needed help to put in world-class processes and computing. Today, it has long surpassed Las Vegas in gambling revenues. Daire also liked Sean for his 'shy, sweet, innocent southern boy' routine that I had already heard forty-three times.

Sean did his thing. Strutting up and down, sucking his teeth just at the right moment to increase the impact of what he was saying and making his well-crafted but seemingly spontaneous jokes. They all loved him by then. It was just at this moment, the moment when victory was within our grasp, that Daire asked his fateful question.

"Well, Sean. You have pointed out our cash management capabilities and areas for improvement but I'm not getting as precise a picture as I'd hope. So just how bad are we at cash management?"

"Well, Daire, the fucking Bank of Pakistan does it better than you."

My experience told me to say something quickly before the stunned silence started to destroy my cardiovascular system.

"Ok gentlemen, let's take a short break, some coffee maybe, and then we'll come back for a final round-up." The thought that Sean should be called an 'insultant' — rather than consultant - flashed through my mind.

Daire took me aside, thanked me for all our efforts over the last two days and said he would be taking the meeting on further without us. The next day, he called me in London to say that they were at the point of feeling "colonised" by us and said they hoped we might help them in future projects... should they arise. He also said that he would be deducting a chunk of our chargeable fees as the NI Regional Manager had found out that one of the junior consultants on the original Branch Performance Improvement project had not completed her consulting education with our company and therefore they didn't believe they should pay for her time as she wasn't properly qualified. He had, indeed, caught me in the long grass. Lions 2 Christians 1.

Epilogue

I bumped into Daire at Heathrow about six months later. He was very warm and complimentary about all the work we had done and how happy he was with the implementation of the changes we had identified and systems that were installed to improve things. He asked what I was working on currently. I told him we were working with a bank in Istanbul. We had projects worth seven million dollars currently and the bank had ambitions to win the "Best Small Bank in Europe" award; a competition which Euromoney ran each year. (This Turkish bank did win the award two years later and also had their transformation written up as a Harvard Business Case Study.) Daire had that same strange one-eyed look on his face as we said our farewells. Lions 2 Christians 2 — final score.

In the mid-2000s, three employees of a Belfast bank were arrested following the identification of £900,000 missing from the incineration records.

I was invited to attend that bank's annual family dinner three months following our last project. Unfortunately, I was already committed to something that day. George Best was to be the guest speaker. He didn't turn up. Apparently, as I was told, George always accepted invitations to after-dinner speeches but sometimes fails to turn up. The bank had paid for his performance in advance, as requested.

Day trip to Brussels

Angie wanted me to tell you that I have had many

incidences on aeroplanes (as you will have had I'm sure). Her favourite is a day trip to Brussels I made in late 1999 — a few years after my experience sitting next to Dr Ian Paisley. I'd caught the short, first flight from Heathrow. Cabin crew threw a free meal at me and collected the debris about (it seemed) 40 seconds later whether you had started on it or not. I had struggled to open the vinaigrette salad dressing the whole time. Just what they were doing serving me a salad at 6:45 am I can't imagine but those were the days when things weren't going well for the "World's Favourite Airline." It must have been the fifteenth different type of condiment packaging I had tried to open that month. These days they are standardised.

On the return trip, I was confronted with another faster-than-the-speed-of-light meal tray. This time we were on hold over Heathrow and had time to savour the meal. I tried to open the vinaigrette salad dressing. I was tired and I just couldn't work it out. Angie would put this down to about four different "disabilities" as she calls them. I must have been struggling with this dressing package for about two minutes when an arm shot across the aisle plucked the offending small package from my mitt, ripped open the top in one easy move and thrust his hand back in front of my nose 'tout suite'. I looked across and saw it was Chris Patten, the last Governor and Commander-in-Chief of Hong Kong. At the time, he was about six months into his appointment as one of the two UK European Commissioners in the EU. At no time did he seem to take his eyes from the paperwork he was reading. His face was slightly puffy and red.

As ever,
Paul

The famous city of Rio de Janeiro

10. Rio and the Bribe
Rio de Janeiro

Dear Brendan,

It was July 1989. I was sitting in my hotel room looking out of the window. There were large trucks, maybe three of them, loading some items lying on Copacabana beach. The Marriott hotel was very well positioned on Copacabana. I'll come back to the trucks later, much later in this story.

Before lunch

I had travelled overnight from New York on Pan Am to

reach Rio, waking after a few hours of dull snoozing in my seat just as the sun came up over the Amazonian forest. For me, on my first visit to South America, the sight was phenomenal. There were trees as far as you could see in any direction. It looked like a green tufted carpet with hidden toys or bric-a-brac under it. There were no gaps or slashes in the carpet. This view went on unchanged for at least two hours. I arrived in a chaotic airport with an assault of noises. Whistles, horns, shouting and a strong hum of many people talking over each other. My suitcase didn't turn up on the carousel. I waited politely until it was obvious it wasn't coming. I walked to the PanAm desk in the baggage hall and explained. The lady looked bored with my situation as if she had dealt with a hundred similar situations that morning. She asked what was in the bag. "Clothes and shoes suitable for business meetings" I blurted, expecting a shrug in return.

I was standing in day-old clothes fit for travel. She said that company policy allowed her to give me US $100 in cash to buy what I needed while they tried reuniting me with my bag which, by the tired tone of her voice, meant "Don't bet on it." Although I knew the $100 was still a useful amount, it would not cover the clothes and suitcase replacement. The situation demanded I just got on with it.

As I was about to exit the baggage hall, I saw my suitcase propped up against a wall. I checked it for damage or missing items but it was in a perfect, unopened condition. I turned to go back to the tired lady. She had shut up the desk, put a closed sign on the counter and had disappeared. I looked around to see that I was the only one left in the hall. Guilt set in.

As the taxi drove me at top speed towards Copacabana, it hit a huge, deep puddle lying in the road and the engine died.

We were sitting in the middle lane of a very fast highway. I spent the next 30 minutes asking if I could get another taxi. The driver was only interested in trying to restart his taxi. It was raining buckets. He was definitely risking his life, but his taxi was his life. It was a yellow Volkswagen Beetle with the front passenger seat missing. A good percentage of taxis were like this at this time in Rio. Through some magic the taxi started again, but coughed and spluttered all the way, finally resting with a fairly loud bang and black smoke at the hotel front door. The door staff were horrified; the driver was crying. I took my bag from the taxi, gave the driver the fare and the Pan Am $100 bill and checked in.

I had arrived in Brazil just as they were having their first free, democratic elections in almost 30 years. There had been a military regime all that time and after about five years of political turmoil, new political parties had formed following multiple demonstrations. I had arrived at a time when Brazilian citizens were able to directly vote for a President.

So, to come back to me sitting in my room looking out of the window and back to the trucks on the beach. From there, I couldn't see properly what they were loading so I picked up the local Rio Marriott courtesy newspaper, English language version. There were many articles covering the elections but one caught my eye. Not only were the people voting for a new President, but they were also voting for local leaders throughout Brazil. In one of the districts/areas of the Amazon, a man was running for office named Ângelo Maldonado Cerqueira de Souza Pedroso. According to the article, Ângelo was a well-known 'ladies' man' and had many offspring from his multiple relationships. He had decided on his election campaign slogan which, when not put into this context wouldn't make sense. "Vote for me, I could be your father," could be seen written on walls, banners, newspaper adverts and the like. I found out later that he won by a landslide. I made a mental note that politics here were a bit different from the United Kingdom.

So by lunchtime, on my first day, on my first visit to South America, I'd had an invaluable induction which prepared me a little for what was to come. The sight from my plane window, the missing suitcase, the taxi ride, the election slogan and the mysterious and incongruous trucks on the beautiful and famous Copacabana beach. What the hell was going to happen next?

After lunch

Long story short, Brazil was part of my 'patch'. My job at the time was to look after an International Account which covered all the activity with this customer, from Canada to Argentina or The Americas as it was grandly called. The term 'looking after' meant the health and wealth of the Corporations relationship with this account. The only specifics were revenue growth which, as I know you would expect, were very specific.

The Brazilian account was centred in São Paulo but first I had to meet the person who "looked after' all International Accounts in Brazil and he lived in Rio de Janeiro. I was a little irritated that I had to meet someone who didn't seem to add anything to what I was there to do but it was expected protocol regardless of whether it made sense. So, I met Josef Santos in the lobby of the Marriott Hotel, as arranged, at two o'clock. It was obvious he was sophisticated, charming, knowledgeable and expensively dressed. He took me to the Rio Yacht Club for pre-drinks drinks. It was my first ever Catuaba. I had asked him for a Caipirinha, but Josef looked at me and said something in a soft voice about how that was considered a beach drink and the special drink of the club was Catuaba which he strongly recommended. It was a gentle way of letting me know that when the waiter came, he didn't want me to commit a social mistake.

Following my arrival experience that morning, I had to mentally pinch myself that I was sitting in an exclusive Yacht Club in Rio de Janeiro drinking Catuaba's with possibly one of the smoothest men in Brazil, if not the planet, who was gracious enough to pretend, almost convincingly, that he was enjoying my company. He gave me comprehensive information about the local account team and what to watch out for; information on the customer and what to watch out for; information about how business was conducted in Brazil and what to watch out for. There was a lot to watch out for I noticed and took notes. We parted after I'd had probably as many Catuaba's in those two hours as I've had since — and that was nearly thirty years ago. I agreed we should meet when I returned from São Paulo to "wrap up the trip." His last words to me were,

"And, Paul, our Corporation absolutely, without question, 100% does not deal with people who require bribes to sign contracts. Remember that." I agreed. It wasn't something I would forget.

São Paulo

The next morning, I flew to São Paulo. I had researched the city and its demographics. I always liked to try and understand what to expect in cultural terms how my customer would operate. Now I look back, I can see I was never successful. Rio was defiantly a very Brazilian city. Very

Latino, vibrant and quite chaotic.

But São Paulo is very different. The official statistics for the metropolitan area are given today as:

6 million of Italian descent

3 million of Portuguese descent

1.7 million of African descent

1 million of Arab descent

665,000 of Japanese descent

400,000 of German descent

250,000 of French descent

150,000 of Greek descent

120,000 of Chinese descent

120,000 to 300,000 Bolivian immigrants

50,000 of Korean descent and

40,000 Jews

I would have liked this information then, in 1989. I was expecting something like Rio, however, more business-like and more Portuguese. The number of Italians as a proportion surprised me, after all the language in Brazil is Portuguese. In Rio, you get the feeling that it is wealth that separates and segments the population. In São Paulo it seems more like race and ethnicity.

I arrived without incident and met the local team. Interestingly, as I arrived at the front of the very large office skyscraper, there were maybe fifty people living in shacks propped up against the front and side of the building. They had donkeys, dogs and horses tied to parts of the building structure. It was so unusual that it was one of my first questions to the small account team. They told me, in a matter of fact way, that they were homeless people with no historical roots or sense of wanting to be somewhere. They were just there living their lives. "But doesn't the Corporation ask the police or some type of authorities to move them?" This would happen in most places I thought. "You move these people and more will come just to fill the gap and take advantage of the site. Our building protects them from the prevailing winds." Fair enough. We talked business and got our customer calling plan together.

I met the customers Financial Executive and Information Technology manager. They were both of Japanese descent and after a very productive two hours, we had the green light to draw up contracts on the sales agreements. They were, however, not yet signed.

Takahiro Watanabe, the Information Technology manager, asked for a separate and private discussion with me.

"OK, Mister Paul, you get what you want? You happy?"

"Yes, I think you should be happy too because we both get what we want and I believe at a fair price."

"I not happy."

"But Takahiro, I don't understand."

"I want know what you do for me."

"Er, for you?"

"Yes. Me. Takahiro. You have competitors. They have something. Want make me happy. You not want make me happy?"

"You mean Takahiro that you want to be personally happy with this deal?" I was over-acting the innocent Englishman abroad.

"Yes, Mister Paul."

I paused for about ten seconds trying to think of my next words. They had to be very well thought out. Our work, proposals and my efforts to come to Brazil could very clearly rest on whether Takahiro could be personally happy! The deal was around $10 million and in 1989 this was a very big deal.

"Takahiro, I have enjoyed your company very much today. I have listened very carefully to everything you have asked, including in our private meeting. Please give me a day or so to come to a conclusion about whether we can find any way to make you happy and that my Corporation will approve. Is that ok?"

"No more than one day, Mister Paul, please."

I debriefed the team back in our office, after slipping through the small homeless village on our way through the front door. After hearing about previous near misses with the law and corruption scandals befalling other companies in Brazil we were all keen to play it straight.

I had a restless night and it wasn't as a result of having a surprisingly good Indian meal with the local team that evening in the city (somewhere). In the morning, the plan was to fly back to Rio, meet Josef, wrap up the trip (as he called it) and fly back to the USA overnight.

The Rio wrap up

I met Josef Santos in his office and told him the whole story.

"Well, congratulations my friend. You have pulled off one of the biggest deals in Brazil we'll have this quarter."

"Not exactly, Josef. As I said, we don't know how we can make Takahiro happy."

"Paul, my dear friend. You're underestimating how we get business done here. Our major competitor, the Japanese firm, have tapped into Takahiro's affinity with his ancestry. They take him to the best Japanese restaurants, they obtain unusual

Japanese antiques which his wife loves to collect and they have interesting banking practices. Takahiro loves their attention and their ability to get items he has been coveting. His salary is good but not at the level which can afford these items. I'm not going to say anything about business practices. Takahiro has, what you say in England, I believe, champagne tastes and beer money."

Wow, I had really underestimated Josef. However, what was our solution that didn't involve bribery? How can we overcome the competition and stay clean? Josef had found out our problem but I already had the feeling he had the solution too.

Josef explained that he had lunch and dinner with Takahiro many times over several years. They didn't talk much about work-related things he said, just about each other.

"I've been waiting to offer him what he wants and I decided that now was the right time to do it. Takahiro's parents came to Brazil almost immediately after the Second World War. They started with nothing. He learnt Japanese from his parents, Portuguese at school and English at university. He saw how hard his parents worked to establish themselves here in Brazil. He also saw how much they missed Japan and the family members they left behind. Brothers, sisters and cousins. Their own parents had passed away. Takahiro's grandfather as a soldier and his grandmother from what could be generalised as poverty."

"So," I said. "He wants something sent over from Japan that he treasures?"

"Ah, close my friend. It's the other way round. He wants to go to Japan to visit the family grave and see his uncles, aunts and cousins who are still alive. His grandmother's ashes are interred in the family grave but not his grandfather. His grandfather was a soldier lost somewhere in the Pacific Islands. He knows he cannot afford to pay for himself just yet but both his wife and Takahiro have been saving hard to make the trip one day. His wife is now very unwell and now it seems she won't ever be able to make the trip..."

I waited for the complete plan as at last, I had caught up with Josef. Well, I thought I had.

"...I have arranged for Takahiro to fly to Tokyo, attend a customer education class at our facility outside of Tokyo. The class is about the software and systems we are proposing in your deal. Everyone wins. He takes as much time before or after the class as his job allows. We pay for the customer's flight, tuition and lodgings as is normal practice in Brazil. He only has to cover the expense outside of the business associated costs and since he will be staying with relatives it will be minimal."

I was about to say something and saw he had more to tell.

"I have called the team in São Paulo to let them know and then I called Takahiro. He was silent for about a minute. He was crying, I could tell, but he could not possibly show that to me. He asked me to stay on the line for a few minutes. When he returned, he had his normal voice and formal manner. He told me that he has a signed contract and asked me to let you know and thank you for all that you have done for him."

Josef smiled and put his hand up to stop my protest. "Paul, that is my job and you did yours."

"But Josef I didn't really do anything."

"Your job was to come here. Pay attention to the customer. Get the business deal set up with Takahiro and the local team. Believe me, just you flying all the way from New York or from wherever you started was enough for the customer to know we take them very seriously. The competition uses local, second-generation Japanese with Takahiro and the Financial Director. They are good but beatable. By the way, I learnt their deal was less expensive than ours so we had to make our deal unbeatable. What is that cliché we hear all the time? Keep your friends close, but your enemies closer."

Josef drove me to the airport as I was flying home to Wilmington, Delaware that night via New York. It was truly ironic that originally, I was reluctant to follow protocol and meet Josef. But without him, I could not have achieved the deal. About half an hour before we arrived at the airport, he asked me if I would do him a favour.

"Of course. How can I help you?"

"Can you please deposit $5,000 cash into my account in the USA for me. The money and the details are in this envelope."

"Of course I can."

It was best not to ask any questions and I knew I could take up to $10,000 into the USA legitimately at that time. It dawned on me that he looked after twelve International Accounts in Brazil similar to mine. I wondered if he asks each account manager flying in and out of Brazil to do him this kind of favour. What was he doing? It was definitely best not to ask. But then I had to say something.

"Josef, this is very flattering. How do you know you can trust me?"

"Because I've seen you. Listened to you. I've seen how you were with Takahiro. It was enough. And of course, I know lots of... er, people in the USA and England... OK, that's a joke."

Well, maybe it was.

The Airport

Rio airport at that time must have had the creepiest flight announcer in the world. She was ultra-slow, with a deep voice and words that seemed to not want to come out into the world. I sat in the Pan Am lounge waiting to hear my flight being slowly called. There was only one other person in the lounge. She was working hard on reports and dictating into a machine (yes, some people still did that in 1989). She broke off her concentration and looked over in my direction. I nodded and said a polite hello. She said hello too and it became obvious she was American. We talked a bit more and I asked her if it was business or pleasure that brought her to Brazil.

She explained that she worked for the US Government and was commissioned to research Brazilian demographics for 1988 or as near as she could get it. The US government apparently wanted to know the profile of the country as it came out of military dictatorship into a democracy. She explained that she did her normal research and got reasonable data and reasonable help. However, she had found out things that troubled her.

"Do you know how big the population is in Brazil today?"

"Erm, no."

"One hundred and sixty million. Do you know how many homeless children there are in Brazil today?"

"A lot. Two hundred thousand? I really have no idea."

"Thirty million."

"But that's not possible surely. Thirty-million, of one hundred and sixty-million are homeless children?"

"Consider that historically most women in Brazil feel

143

their main purpose in life is to reproduce. They have very strong Catholic roots with a mixture of African influences such as Candomblé and Umbanda. These religions all celebrate procreation. That and the relatively high death rates in babies and children has led to very large but poor families. Children have by necessity looked after themselves and each other. Children drift away from their homes and form groups which develop strong bonds. They look for, and find, food together. They live anywhere that is safe but part of a group. Older children develop the group into a gang. These can be very dangerous. Thirty-million is obviously a guess but an educated guess. Most of the data come from the Military regime itself, what little they bothered to collect. They didn't care about it and were certainly not embarrassed."

I did find the numbers hard to believe. However, since then I've seen quite a few TV programmes about 'street children' all over Latin America. On my last trip to Brazil the following year, I was attacked by a gang of about twenty children, ages probably between six and sixteen, on a quiet Sunday morning as I walked from my hotel to a marketplace. As they came at me, I ran at them shouting and screaming. This unsettled them and they scattered long enough for me to run back to the hotel and get a taxi. Everyone is afraid of a madman.

I remember, at the airport, the American woman explaining how local and tourist police were paid by government agencies to get rid of the gangs of children, particularly in high, lucrative tourist areas. Ipanema and Copacabana beaches in particular. She explained that 'to get rid of' meant kill. It would happen almost always at night and they would tidy up in the morning.

"I saw large trucks on Copacabana on my first morning

here. Was that anything to do with what you are telling me?"

She nodded.

As ever,

Paul

PS: I went to Brazil twice more in the same job. My second trip had none of the above incidents but was truly memorable in other ways.

PPS: Japanese immigrants were encouraged by the Brazilian Government by way of grants and loans to start life again following the Second World War. Brazil needed cheap labour for agriculture. They mainly settled in São Paulo where commerce experienced strong growth.

PPPS: Takahiro had a wonderful trip to Japan.

PPPPS: Josef, I found out later, had been raised by a wealthy family and had been educated mainly in the USA, which is why his English was so good. He retired three years after I had met him. He bought a house and moved to Connecticut.

PPPPPS: I believe Brazil has improved on the number of homeless children since 1989 with recent 'official' numbers ranging between 200,000 and 8 million. It is difficult to judge without independent validation. However, judging from the number of politicians arrested for corruption, Brazil has retained many of the questionable business practices.

PPPPPPS: I read something a street-child had said which I felt explains their lives much better than I could ever do.

"We sniff glue because we need to. We steal watches, necklaces, earrings. We don't have anywhere to eat, we don't have anywhere to sleep, we don't have anywhere to stay, that's why we steal. I steal, I walk around, I sniff glue, and then I can't do anything. I haven't got a Dad — he died seven years ago. I have eight brothers and sisters but I can't really stay at home, so I live on the street. That's how I lead my life."

11. The unobservant consultant and the unidentified briefcase South Africa

Dear Brendan,

I was met from the overnight flight at Johannesburg airport by Otis Hemingway. Otis was African-American, mid-forties, and very charming. His job was to establish consulting and services for the Corporation as a viable business in South Africa. He was two and a half years into a three-year assignment away from his home base in Atlanta, Georgia and having a difficult time. My boss had suggested, correction, told me to help him.

Otis briefed me as we drove to the business district in downtown. I had various internal meetings (God knows why) and a series of customer meetings both here and in Cape Town where someone else would escort me around. I liked Otis but I was bored with the familiar complaining tones of people who are trying to make change happen. This was my first time in South Africa and I was more interested in the landscape and the 'High Veldt' as we drove. Johannesburg sits high up on the central plateau and is surrounded by huge, sweeping savannah (Veldt). It was July, therefore winter, and the light was clear, soft and colours vibrant. The air was cool but not cold. The long swirling, golden and light brown grass was speckled with local figures walking along the road and through the terrain. We passed through the scruffy, urban beginnings of Jo'burg. Concrete shells housed tiny businesses; greengrocers, second-hand clothing, garage mechanics, bicycle shops, furniture sellers and more. We arrived in the business sector, known as the Central Business District (CBD). It was like any business district that you will find in any medium-sized North American city. Skyscrapers and high rise office blocks. The streets were busy with largely white, European looking people going about their business. There were stretches of lovely gardens or beautiful grassy areas where I noticed shabbily clothed black men standing alone, hardly moving. They were like statues. Typically, they had nothing with them, no bags, no bikes, nothing. Just standing around, not obviously connected to anything or anyone. We entered the giant office building and started a long day of work.

Around four-thirty in the afternoon, the local staff started clearing away and it was obvious they were finishing for the day.

"Otis, what's happening?"

"It's nearly five and we all want to be gone shortly. So I'll take you to your hotel and we can start tomorrow at nine."

"Otis, now don't get me wrong, but do you always finish work so early?" I had not had a nine to five job for nearly thirty years.

"Paul, we're in Jo'burg. Everyone in the business area leaves around five to ensure we are out of the city by sundown and safely in our homes or bars or restaurants in safer parts of the city. Believe me, you should not be in this part of town after dark."

On the way to Sandton, the 'safer' part of the city, he told me that safety had become such a problem that there had been a large exodus of financial and commercial firms from the area and this was rapidly increasing. The city had become crime-ridden and I had noticed that most small talk that day had been about the level of crime. Petty crime, break-ins and violent crime.

During my visit, a customer told me his house had been burgled three times. His insurance company told him that unless he installed the latest security equipment (recommended by them) they would no longer insure him. He dutifully installed it all. The following week he left his house first thing in the morning to go to work and his house was burgled by ten o'clock that morning. The burglars had entered the gated community, climbed on his roof, waited and watched him leave for work and then took tiles off the roof and entered that way, turning off the various alarms as they crept through the house.

"But you live in a gated community with armed gatekeepers. How is that possible?" I had asked him.

He looked at me as if to say, 'you idiot'.

"Because the security guards are not paid very much. Burglars pay more and have ways of intimidating them that aren't in the security company's managers manual." I felt like an idiot.

As we drove to my hotel, I asked Otis about the men standing like statues in various places as we passed by.

"They stand there because these were the places that were just not available to them under the apartheid system. It was "Whites Only." They just enjoy doing something that they weren't allowed to do before. It's an expression of freedom." We went over arrangements for the next day and I hit the sack early.

Paying attention does help

The next day went well. I met a customer executive and he seemed to like what I had to say. It went well to the point we were talking about when we would start work with them, how big the project was going to be and quite a detailed plan. This almost never happens so quickly. I was delighted and felt good about myself. Otis, who had sat with us all day, had a fairly shocked look on his face. Somewhere deep down his inner smile must have been shining through, but it wasn't obvious. The customer looked at me and said, "OK, this was a good session for both of us, so how about we go for a drink?"

Otis, still with a fairly frozen look on his face, declined because of some other commitment. You'll find out later why he did. Arrangements were made for contracts to be drawn up, something that Otis would take the lead on, and my job was to start thinking about skills, people and what previous projects we had done in a similar vein.

The customer drove me to a bar. He insisted on covering all the expenses for the evening and we basically talked through the whole project, setting expectations on both sides. He then suggested dinner in a restaurant close to the bar and about three miles from my hotel. More drinks and a splendid meal were provided by a very busy and meticulous establishment. My customer was showing strong signs that he liked me and the project we had shaped. Then his phone rang.

His phone lay on the table and I noticed the name 'Nigel' on the screen as it was ringing. The conversation went like this.

"Oh, hello darling. How was your day?"

Silence while he listened. "Oh, I'm sorry to hear that."

The tone of the conversation was of a close couple sharing what had happened that day. Trying not to show I was taking notice of their intimacy, I glanced around the restaurant, killing time. The scales fell from my eyes. I hadn't noticed a lot of things that suddenly were blindingly obvious. The restaurant was full of men. Customers, waiters and bar staff. I recalled our waiter being quite friendly and flirtatious with my customer and curiously teasing to me. We were very definitely in a gay man's restaurant or club or some such and I was in a situation I both had no experience of before and no idea what was an appropriate way to conduct myself as a non-gay bloke. What's more, should I way up if my customer's interest in our project was laced with other motivations? I was out of my depth and, although ridiculous, felt surprisingly vulnerable. I recalled the look on Otis's face as he left for his evening (somewhere else). Was this some kind of set up? Am I overreacting to an unfamiliar situation? I decided what to do.

After a further few minutes my customer was wrapping up his conversation. "OK then sweetheart, see you tomorrow and travel home safely."

I yawned hard. "You're going to have to forgive me but I've ordered a taxi to take me to my hotel. I'm really knackered… (notice I chose to use a word that tried — pathetically — to be a non-gay word)… and need to get a better night's sleep than I've had for the last two nights or I'm going to turn into a pumpkin." (I regretted that last word).

He looked devastated. "But Paul, I thought we could go back to my place to continue our project discussions, have a little cognac and relax."

"Jim, I'm really sorry. I need to be fresh if I'm going to do my best for you tomorrow and get the work done in the time available. Please understand."

The taxi turned up. I arrived at my hotel in less than ten minutes. I slept rather fitfully if I remember correctly. I was very annoyed with myself for not being a very observant person which put my customer and me into an awkward situation. I made several mental notes to myself during the fitful night to have a little chat with Otis in the morning.

Otis called my room around 8:30 am and dropped a bomb. He told me that the plan for the day had been changed by the customer. He no longer wished to see me to settle any more detail. The customer had re-arranged his day to do other things. At this point, I thought my worst fears were being realised. Otis then started talking about the next customer in another company we were due to meet and try to win a project with them. He briefed me in detail over the phone about how we should treat the customer and the meeting. Just before he was about to hang up I felt I had to say something.

"Otis, I'm sorry. I really screwed things up yesterday. I just hadn't, er, er, read the, er, how shall I describe it… I hadn't read the customer or situation very well and it obviously is disastrous for you now."

He laughed loudly and then it turned into a squeaky laugh like you do when it's a really uncontrolled belly laugh. You would have liked Otis a lot.

"Hey man, relax. Congratulations. He signed the contract first thing this morning. He wants us to start before the end of the month and he wants you to be the Quality Assurance executive. It's our first project of this kind over here and I think my boss is going to love me. Yours will probably love you too." I thought, hmmm, fat chance.

"Otis, old bean. Would you kindly let me know of all

relevant information, er you know, er, things I should take into account about our customers before I meet them even if you think they're extraneous? Things could have turned out very differently last night you bugger. Oh, please pardon the expression." This made Otis start laughing even harder. English phrases made him laugh but I sensed he was in really deep chuckle mode and was picturing the broader landscape.

My business endeavours were pretty routine and uneventful for the rest of the trip. A few seeds were planted and follow up meetings for local executives and project leaders were fixed. I was there to pique interest. I enjoyed Cape Town. An extremely scenic city from almost any angle. In my experience, second only to Rio de Janeiro.

I visited one insurance customer who had more than seven thousand people on-site. It was like a small town. This organisation was a complete contradiction in opportunity terms. Both very unpromising, but our biggest prospect. The obstacle was an Englishman. Probably in his late thirties, Eton educated and had his head firmly up his own arse (in my humble opinion). He didn't like me. During the first conversation we had, I could feel him switching off. His irritation came from the answer I gave about which school I had attended and this put me, and therefore all that I could bring to his firm, somewhere between "You're wasting my time" and "Get out of my office now!" I nearly told him that the fact that he went to a very expensive, elite and successful school didn't matter to me. I wouldn't hold it against him. Afterwards, I really wish I had.

I thought of who in my organisation had gone to Eton. It was Julian Leg, recently hired as an MBA graduate from Oxford and not yet experienced enough to deal with the likes of this gentleman. In my trip report summary, I stated that the customer wasn't ready for us yet. My boss thought that was my fault and I suppose that's true.

Blue sky reports

Fred Bouchard was hard-nosed and unreasonably irritable. He was one of my most knowledgeable and insightful experts but not a leader of people. He had led people before, in the US Army, unsuccessfully. He was a young lad when he trained to be a sniper. His job was to get ahead of the platoon to seek enemy snipers, booby traps and in general anything that threaten him and his comrades. He had undertaken many of these critically important missions before he was shot. He was seen by an enemy sniper a split second before he'd seen him. The enemy was sitting fifty feet up a tree directly across from him. One bullet passed through a leg and one clipped a kidney. He told me that he'd fallen out of the tree, picked up by his platoon, taken to a hospital in Saigon and eventually flown back to the USA. He would never say how many of his platoon were killed, injured or otherwise and he would never talk about his own exploits with a gun. His irritability was famous in our team but he didn't care. It was worse when he had been drinking. Customers loved him mostly but he would overstep his (how shall I put this) direct, and to the point, style. I liked him a lot because he helped enormously in winning business and delivering hard messages to customers who needed to listen and take action. He also told the team very funny jokes.

Fred was our most senior person on the Jo'burg project — secured during my now famously awkward dinner date. Part of our approach in our international projects was to get experts like Fred to combine with local Corp staff (to build experience and expertise) and customer employees (a selling point on building their own experience and expertise). Being the most senior doesn't always mean leader on our projects and we had someone from London head it up. Gordon Mitchell was a dour and severe Scotsman and appointed project leader.

Gordon's main skills were project structure, management and discipline. He found Fred bewildering. Fred had none of his skills which made him a perfect match as far as I was concerned. As long as they respected each other it would work and encouraged by me they worked very hard at respecting each other until the last day of the project. Following the final and successful presentation of our work to my customer friend and his executives, our team headed for the exit. At the building's reception, Fred wanted to go back to see someone who he had liked and particularly valued in the project work and asked Gordon to look after his brief/suitcase. It had Fred's laptop, reports and personal effects, untidily stuffed inside no doubt.

While he was waiting for Fred to come back, Gordon decided to pop into the Gents. He was just exiting the toilet when the building alarm sounded. Everyone had to evacuate immediately to a nearby car park and await further instructions. Our project group collected together waiting to see how quickly things would clear up. "We get this often these days as we are threatened quite frequently by all kinds of organisations," a customer told us. "We even have to call in the army sometimes." Five minutes later, a South African army helicopter swooped down by the front of the building, picked up something on a hook at the end of a long metal cord and flew off to a nearby field. Fred shouted, "That's my ******* suitcase you Scottish ****." As we all stared at the unfolding drama of Fred's suitcase, it was blown up. We saw bits of paper, metal and clothing littering the landscape as they fluttered down onto the Veldt.

Fred and Gordon didn't work together ever again. I took great care about that.

As ever,

Paul

12. The loneliness of the long-distance meeting
New York

Dear Brendan,

Tom Delano had no discernible sense of humour. The only thing that amused him was seeing someone else have bad luck or any kind of misfortune. In Europe, we'd call it schadenfreude. He was 100% a New Yorker. Personally, I liked the people I had met who were brought up in the New York and New Jersey area. I'd worked with quite a few of them when we lived in Delaware. They are very distinct Americans. And Tom was definitely a 'no shit kinda guy'. Taking prisoners did not fit in his modus operandi. He truly didn't understand why it would. He didn't take prisoners but he did collect friends.

Territory trespassing

Tom came to visit me in London because he wanted to know what I was up to. It was early December. Later, he told me he'd never been outside of the USA and barely outside of New York and New Jersey, so it made his visit to my London office even more remarkable. He walked in as though he owned the building, the city and everyone in it. He had that kind of demeanour. He sat down without saying anything to

157

start with. He just looked at me. I, of course, knew who he was. An entry in my diary had been made a few days before and I'd heard of him through some work we were doing with an American bank in the UK. He was the International Account Executive for that bank and was responsible for the health and wealth of the relationship between our company and that bank.

"So you're Clutterbuck, right?" he said with all the words rolled into one and barked out loud. Loud was to be the best way to describe his side of our discussion.

Now humour is, in general, a good thing as long it's in context and will be understood. It seemed to work well for me mostly I thought (although in hindsight it mostly was a big mistake). Nevertheless, I thought I'd break the ice a little with Tom. At that time, it was well known in the office that some New Yorkers were able to fabricate a business reason to come to London during December and bring their wives along.

"Good to meet you, Tom. Just over for some Christmas shopping?" I jested. Big mistake.

"What the fuck you talkin' about? Let's cut the crap. What are you doin' in my account?" he bellowed. I closed my office door.

I gave him the background and people involved in a large project I was responsible for with the American bank in question. The project was underway and was gaining ground and achieving its objectives one-by-one. He didn't take notes.

"So, how much stuff you gonna stuff in this project?" he less than gently enquired. By 'stuff' he meant products. Hardware and software are 'stuff' in this context. Tom was a traditional stuff salesman and he got where he was by selling boatloads of 'stuff' to anyone who was looking, and quite a few who weren't looking. Obviously, he was considered good at his job.

"Tom, this is initially a service we're providing. As I've just told you, essentially the project is about using what we know to improve customers performance at what they do. Opportunities for 'stuff' will no doubt happen as we go through the work they are paying for." I was thinking of drawing big pictures on my office whiteboard to explain but I'd already used humour badly.

After a difficult twenty minutes, he gave up on his insistence of having 'stuff' planned and force-fitted no matter how the project shaped for the customer. He started asking questions about the people working with us from the customer. He was overly inquisitive about the head of the business who had bought our project services, John White, our main sponsor.

Having apparently got all the information he wanted, except how much 'stuff' we were going to sell directly as a result of the project, he got out of his seat and walked out of my office. I didn't see him again until much later in this story.

During lunch, I thought about how someone could be an International Account Executive and basically not travel outside their US State, let alone their country. He must do a lot of telephone/videoing work and emails. So why didn't he just pick up the phone and call me for the information he wanted? And didn't get. Had he only travelled to understand how much 'stuff' would be sold as a result of our project? I didn't think so. Was I treading on 'his' territory? So what was it? I didn't like the smell of it. Mostly, I didn't like him not smiling at my Christmas shopping jest. I thought he needed to 'lighten up'!

The telephone call

Two days later my boss called me. He'd had a telephone

call at 11 pm the previous evening from the boss of our New York banking sector. He'd forgotten there was a time zone difference, well, actually he didn't care to be more precise. I got the drift. I was to fly to New York the next day, go to a strange-sounding hotel for the night, make a presentation of the bank project, early the next morning, to the Information Technology Board of our customer and fly back overnight. Basically, catch a plane to New York and catch the same plane the next day back and, while I'm at it, make friends with a fairly senior group of customers who make very big decisions about the business between our companies. I was beginning to regret having won this large project which, at the time, was considered a breakthrough with this customer. C'est la vie, mon brave.

The plane was packed. The only seat was in economy class at the front of a block of seats at the back of the plane. A toilet block was in front of my face and the wall had a baby changer shelf that could be lowered down for nappy/diaper changing. It was in keeping with the rest of this experience that I sat in the middle of a group of forty Hasidic people travelling back to New York. It was as though I was invisible to everyone, including the cabin crew for the next seven hours. At the end of the flight, a cabin crew member asked me to stay in my seat until everyone else had 'de-planed'. Then, as I made my way off, all of the crew gave me a round of applause and handed me a bottle of Champagne. Nothing was said. It had been an unusual experience, as clearly, I had annoyed the group by my presence among them. They changed babies under my nose, reached across me to one another, shouted and spilt liquid over me while I was trying to sleep/ read/watch a film and frequently press the attendant button, without an answer. Let's just say it was difficult for all concerned.

Following instructions I had been given, and a Rand McNally map (no Sat/ Nav in those days) bought at the car hire desk, I drove along Long Island for about an hour and a half. I came to where I was staying. It was a mansion house, set back from the main road and similar to the 17th century architecture of most Manor houses in Britain. It was fairly dark as I drove along the long, winding driveway to the car park adjacent to the house. One dim light shone through the front door guiding me to a large, old oak desk behind which was sitting a well-dressed bald man resembling the TV and Film actor Telly Savalas. He just looked at me, with dark blue rings under his eyes, expecting me to speak first.

"Good evening," I said in a pleasant voice hoping this would be enough for him to not murder me immediately. "I hope I've found the right place." I went on to explain who I was, why I was there and who invited me. I explained that a reservation had been made for me to stay the night, although I admit there had been a hint of a question in my delivery. 'Telly' said nothing. He handed me a door key with a numbered fob, pointed to a very dimly lit lift (I think that it was spelt 'elevator') door. No request for credit cards, or proof of who I was. I stopped myself saying, "Hey, baldy, cat got your tongue?" as I had a strong feeling that he would, in fact, get my tongue using scissors or a blunt knife. I took the lift to the only other floor. The lights in the corridor were motion sensitive and I found a door number that coincided with the key fob.

It was fairly obvious that I was the only guest in the place that night. Igor, or whatever his name was, either slept in a coffin in the basement or went home to the Bride of Dracula.

I was dog tired. The time difference between New York and London was five hours, but the good news was I could consider tomorrows 9:00 am meeting start a bonus as that would be 2:00 pm for my mind and body. I like to look on the bright side, even if there isn't one available. It was midnight when I fell asleep and 3 am when I woke, never to go back to sleep again that night. Ah, ok but that meant I had six hours to prepare for my meeting. Looking on the bright side. I was feeling incredibly hungry. I had nothing since leaving London. Nothing on the plane for reasons already explained. Nothing on arrival or journey in the car. Nothing offered at check-in. I picked up the phone and dialled, yes that's right, dialled zero for an operator or Igor's front desk. No answer.

I was dressed in my best business clothes at 8:00 am. I had rehearsed my presentation about three times, a healthy number which made me think hard about the high level of interruptions, questions and what hidden motives the attendees have had for hauling me over to New York in this manner. I went down the stairs rather than the lift as it was a better way of getting me going physically. I was feeling sluggish and very hungry. No Igor at the desk but there was a large notice, presumably for me, describing how to get to the meeting room. I could smell breakfast had been laid out in the room as I approached. A smartly dressed man of about thirty greeted me and thanked me for coming. He asked me to "Please wait over there on the sofa. Thank you." Bugger, no breakfast. So here I was, really hungry, unbelievably tired and entering a hostile environment. At least, it seemed hostile the way all this had happened. My intuition was right.

I was called in at 9:05 am. I could see and smell the buffet breakfast at the back of the room. Quickly looking around I saw about a dozen men sitting round a large oak table that seated them all comfortably, with room to spare. The boss sat in a bigger chair than the rest at the head of the long table. His name was Tony Grasso. Next to him, on his right side was sitting, I was shocked to see, my new best friend Tom Delano. As I greeted them all with a (nervous) smile and a cheerful British "Good Morning," I looked briefly at each one to make eye contact. As I went around some were mumbling a "Hi how are ya?" or "How ya doin?" but most said nothing. Of the twelve, some were tall and big, some short and fat, some grey-haired, some dark-haired but all had a Mediterranean look. Tony Grasso was one of the smallest, with dark (dyed) hair and was fatter than most. He greeted me with, "Clutterbuck, right?"

At this point, I want to pause. I want to tell you a separate story that was running through my mind as I slowly went around the table shaking hands. It will help you sense the ambience of the meeting room I was standing in.

Louie the Leg Breaker

My friend Carl, was a salesman in the early seventies in New York City. He had a set of unconnected, medium-sized customers to sell his company's products, driven by an annual quota. It was a simple system. A range of products matched against a list of customers; on-your-marks-get-set-go. Carl was good at his job and, by and large, his customer set bought his products in the right quantities and he made his sales targets every year.

Then his company changed the system. The unpaid debt was rising and the 'Accounts Receivable' department was struggling. Cash flow was becoming a big problem. So, of course, his company calculated debt limits for each customer and charged the salesforce with keeping debt below a certain number, setting debt targets in the same way as they set sales targets.

Zenon Zaborski was the CEO of one of Carl's customers. Debt levels had regularly been above the limit set for Zenon's company. Carl had been given a kindly word by his boss, and, I'm paraphrasing, what I'm told he said to Carl. It was along the lines of "Get the fuck out this office, go and see that tight-fisted S.O.B. and get our money. Don't come back until you have his cheque, or knowing him, cash. Tell him I'm fed up with his yada, yada, yada about the sixteen reasons he can't pay this month. This will cost you real money if he doesn't pay up!"

Carl talked to Zenon's secretary and fixed an appointment. Zenon was a worldly man. In his late fifties and a Brooklyn businessman through and through. He'd grown up in Brooklyn and came from a regular, poor Brooklyn family. Zenon had built his business from nothing and, if he had sold it, the value would be probably about two million dollars at that time. He was lean, grey, tallish and dressed in clothes that were brand new, eight years previously. He had an unusual Brooklyn accent which had a slight, discernible Polish tinge.

He greeted Carl like an old friend. They sat together and Zenon poured them both some Polish tea. It was Figura Tea imported from the 'mother' country. Zenon said he needed a diet supplement with senna extract. Apparently, he had told Carl, it helped women get slimmer and healthier. "It is also very helpful with constipation and ingestion." He'd explained he'd bought it in bulk, mainly for use by his wife. However, it was useful to have in the office to offer friends like Carl. They discussed the debt situation and, as Carl looked over his A4 notepad at Zenon, he started to tick off the excuses he was hearing from the other side of the desk. Zenon, on this occasion, only gave five excuses. Carl started to open up on the situation and suggest ways in which Zenon could overcome his obstacles to paying up. Carl drank his tea and looked at Zenon, waiting for the next move. Zenon merely poured Carl another cup of Figura. The polite but firm discussion from both sides on this subject was broken after about fifteen minutes by Zenon who asked Carl to come back the same time next week and he should have the cheque for him. Carl looked at him in disbelief that he had used excuse number twelve and it was a fob-off. Even after Carl had explained that his boss would most likely deduct pay from him as a result of going back empty-handed, Zenon just sympathised and re-emphasised his own problems. Impasse.

Carl thanked the secretary on his way out. He got in his car and started to think hard. What to do next? As he drove through Brooklyn, he had a really hot sensation in the pit of his stomach. Sweat broke out on his forehead. He needed a toilet urgently. Seeing a restaurant/bar along the street he pulled over, parked and, keeping his knees close together, minced inside. He saw the sign 'Men' and dived in. A full fifteen minutes went by before Carl felt safe enough to re-emerge. He sat at the bar, asked for a bourbon, downed it and asked for a second. He had been sitting quietly on the bar stool for about an hour trying to work out how to get through this situation.

It was quiet in the bar area and Carl was the only person there until a small, dark-haired man sat on the stool next to him. After a while, the small, Italian looking man turned to him and said, "Hey, how ya doin'" He was a confident man who had inquisitive eyes. They swapped New York pleasantries and the new bar customer asked what he was doing there, in this part of Brooklyn, in the middle of the afternoon. Carl turned to look at him. He looked about forty, but probably younger, and had a very short neck, almost no neck. It was a very noticeable feature. Carl explained about Zenon, his job and how he needed to get the debt cleared between his company and Zenon.

"OK, pal. Here's what ya gonna do. Ya go back to this guy, ya gonna give him this card and say ya got five minutes to wait for the cheque and then ya gonna have to leave. This guy is gonna pay. Believe me. Hey, take my $100 bill. If he pays, you came back here with my $100. If he doesn't pay ya still gonna come back here with my $100. Deal?" Carl didn't know what to make of this, particularly the need for him to take $100 and then return it. But the several bourbon drinks were beginning to kick in. He left the bar and drove back to Zenon Zaborski's office. His secretary said she couldn't let him in to see Zenon as he didn't have an appointment and Zenon was very particular about who he spends time with out-of-the-blue. Carl asked if she could take a calling card into Zenon and tell him he would be just outside his office, but will only wait five minutes for a cheque and then he will have to leave. As Carl handed the card to her, he noticed it just said "Louie" with a telephone number. Zenon came out of his office about two minutes later and rapidly handed over a cheque. "Excuse me, Carl, I didn't realise you knew Louie the Leg Breaker." The cheque was for the full amount of debt outstanding. Carl took it and left. He met Louie still sitting on the same stool. "Thank you, Louie, you really saved my day, to say the least. Here is your $100 and I'd like to add another $100."

"OK, I accept ya offer my friend. Yoose can keep the card as fair exchange. If you wanna anodder it'll cost ya anodder $100 each time, so I'd use it and hang on to it, if I was yoose. Know what I mean? If anyone ya know has the same situation as yoose did, call the number and I'll get a card to 'em. Same price." Louie got up without paying his bill and walked out.

The boss was delighted with Carl when he arrived back in the office. Zenon was never late paying his bills again. Through Carl, Louie made quite a bit of loose change in the next year or two from his calling card business. The unsettled debt in that part of the city improved enormously in the following two years.

"Who should I fire? Is it gonna be you?"

The point of that side story was to help you picture Tony Grasso and five other members of the twelve sitting around the table and whose hands I was shaking. All five could have been 'Louie the Leg Breaker'. I couldn't get the story out of my mind.

The ones that caught my eye, were short, overweight, olive-skinned with very short necks. "Well, my friend. Start talking about your project in dear old England," said Tony Grasso with a heavily nasal tone of voice.

Before leaving London, I obviously had talked with my project manager who was leading the team full time on the customer site so I felt clued up. I used overhead projection and spoke clearly. I asked for questions whenever they wanted to ask. None were forthcoming. The whole time I talked, my 'colleague', Tom Delano, spoke quietly in Tony's ear. Nobody else even lifted a coffee cup. After about thirty minutes Tony held up his hand to stop me mid-sentence.

"OK, so what I see here is a buncha guys not performing. You got your numbers comparing deese guys in England with stuff from other banks from, like, all around da world and in da States too and my guys don't even come close to bein' da best at what they do. Right? And I get that they ain't da best at keeping real cheap. So what I want to know, Clutterbuck, is, who should I fire?"

I blabbed on about questions like that were not in the scope of the project; we couldn't possibly comment of the banks own personnel employment decisions; these decisions were entirely for our customers; our job was to assess performance and compare to others doing the same work and recommend what action to take with a plan to carry it out.

"Choozkiddinme. Look Clutterbuck, let's cut da crap. Do I wanna fire John White?" His strong native accent was emerging, not a good sign.

"As I said, Mister Grasso, our company has not been employed to make recommendations on our customer's personnel being fit for their positions." I held as firm as I could, given the fairly short and to the point opponent. I looked briefly at my 'colleague' Tom Delano. His face was motionless, his eyes unblinking, his body tense.

"Well, who should I fire? Is it gonna be yoose? Da way I see it, we're payin' you alodda denaro to come up wid solutions to our problems at dat place in good old England. We got problems, big problems down there. Tell me, should I fire that son-of-a-bitch?"

"Firstly, Mister Grasso I want to make it clear that we are confident that all the problems will be fixable and we will lay out a plan to do that. The vast majority, given the right focus, and I know that you will be focussed, will be solved within six months." I looked at Tom Delano in vain.

"Seems to me that firing John White will be da answer to alodda deese problems but you're not telling me how to solve dat particular problem are you? So as part of your plan, I wanna see what action I should take to fix John White! If I don't see that, we ain't payin' no invoice from yoose." His native accent was emerging again. Again, not a good sign. I suddenly realised what the purpose was of getting me urgently in front of this meeting.

Well, you will be getting the impression by now that he was definitely putting the squeeze on me about John White! John was our sponsor for this project, it was highly profitable work and we were doing a good job as far as we could tell; up to now, that was. If I told Grasso to fire, or even not to fire John White, I was pretty sure I'd be breaking our internal Business Conduct Guidelines at a minimum, and that would definitely have consequences for me. I would probably not be breaking the local employment laws but I didn't know that for sure. This is New York. I'm not from New York. What I was sure about is that it would have huge implications for our business. Word would get around that we were in the business of assessing customer personnel and making recommendations about their performance. In this particular situation, it was being clearly put. Should John White keep his job? Grasso was certainly chomping at the bit to get rid of John White, perhaps there was more to it than I knew. It certainly felt like it. So, what to say next?

"Mister Grasso, what I can do for you right now, if you'll allow me a five-minute break, is provide you with the information on what to do." I calmly stated.

"Right, Clutterbuck. Yoose got five." Tony Grasso said at high volume his head turned as he stood up but I still didn't see much neck. Tom Delano was enjoying my situation. Nice guy.

I opened my laptop, connected to our database, found what I was looking for and made the page full screen for projection. I then thought through how to conduct the next half an hour or so. After four minutes of the allotted five, I notified Tony I was ready when he was. They all sat down.

"All our clients want us to put the solution to their problems in their own hands," I declared. Firm-ground so far but I was sweating inside. So, what I have projected up on the screen for you all to see is the criteria for the skills and experience required, in our opinion given our world-wide skills database, for a very large Banking Data Centre executive." The list was extensive on the left-hand margin. Across the top was typed the different scale of support the Data Centre reached. For example: "One geographical area" such as North East USA and then "USA Wide" followed by "International" meaning two or more countries on the same continent and finishing with 'Global'.

"This graphic comes from our extensive, worldwide experience of Data Centre managers we choose internally, combined with those of our customers." I thought that was a knockout line of defence but nobody moved a muscle. Not even in their faces, which all stared at me with unblinking eyes.

"What I propose we do is either I lead the discussion with the whole room on John White's capabilities against this criteria and score it as we go through, or I leave while you discuss this among your good selves or, Mister Grasso, you might choose to assess this privately yourself. Going through this exercise will enable you to decide whether John White should stay in his job." I was calm and ready for another twist.

"So, Clutterbuck yoose ain't gonna tell me da fire him?" His head turned slowly both ways as the rest of his body was entirely still. He was trying to sense the mood of the room. He glared at me. The intensity was at an extreme level, certainly for me.

"I've known John for two months, I understand that John has been in this job for four years now. I really do believe you can assess his capabilities significantly better than me." We were now at the point of who was going to blink first. If I gave a public opinion like this, one way or the other, I would be the loser. So I had nothing to lose by putting the ball back in his court.

Tom Delano whispered in Tony Grasso's ear for about thirty-seconds. A very long time. A very, very long time. Tony got up, came round the beautiful oak table, grabbed my hand and shook it twice and said. "Thank you. Useful. We gonna carry on widout ya now, so gitattaheer"

On my way out, I asked Tom Delano to call me as soon as he had a chance.

I was starving. I'd get something at the airport I thought. There was a nightmare traffic holdup on the Belt Parkway into JFK Airport. I just had time to check-in and go to the gate for my flight to London. The woman who checked me in asked: "How was your day so far, sir?" At that point, I found out something new about myself. I had more self-control than I thought I had. Also, something else new happened. I really, really enjoyed my inflight meal for the only time on record.

as ever,
Paul

PS: Tom Delano called me two weeks later. He confirmed that the only reason I had been "requested" to attend the meeting with Tony Grasso was to give a reason to fire John White and I was to be the useful tool with which to do it. I was supposed to be the tool. However, I'd been successful in giving Tony a reason, but not as planned. Despite me not answering his question about firing John White, I had given him a template to use for that purpose and he duly filled in (manipulated) my matrix, showed how John was not up to the job and had something to justify his action inside the bank. He was very pleased with my contribution and I had escaped the personal consequences. It's a funny old world.

PPS: In the conversation with Tom Delano he revealed that he had grown up with Tony Grasso. They were best buddies and looked out for each other.

PPPS: I also learned that John White had previously been Tony Grasso's boss. There had been an incident between them a long time before and Tony was settling a score. Three weeks after our project finished, John White was re-assigned to the Caribbean to be in charge of all the bank branches in the region. A job from which he retired, happily.

PPPPS: We won four more contracts from that area of the banks business and the most senior person to sign off those contracts in the bank was… guess who? Yes, Tony Grasso.

PPPPPS: There is a bit of "All's well that ends well" in this story. However, there is something else to come out of the "Louie The Leg Breaker" anecdote. Following the meeting my friend had with Louie in the early 1970s, Carl had thought no more about it. In 2015, Carl saw a newspaper article reporting an alleged scam to do with car dealerships in New Jersey shopping malls. The owner of one Mall, of particular interest to the Police Organised Crime Unit, was Louis Gambini Jr. and, as it happens, the son of Louis "Louie the leg-breaker" Gambini Sr. who was also on the payroll of the Mall between 2003 to 2007. The newspaper report suggested that father and son had "ties to the mob." Carl thought that having the right calling card can help a lot.

Gaucho and horse

13. An Argentinian Gaucho named Bruno
Buenos Aires

Dear Brendan,

I don't know whether you still have a concept of inflation in heaven. This next story for you is set in Argentina in 1989. The country had record inflation of 4,923.3 (let's just call it 5,000) per cent when I arrived in Buenos Aires, in July that year. The year after I was there, early in 1990, inflation reached 8,000 per cent.

My arrival

What is it like to be a citizen in a country with 5,000 per cent inflation? On my first full day, on my way to the office with the local team, I noticed long queues of people on the streets. I knew that the country was going through high inflation but I didn't realise it was at the hyper level. I assumed, wrongly, that the queues were for bread, meat and other basic necessities. I had seen that in East Berlin in 1979 where they not only had high inflation but a shortage of products and commodities. I had been told it was easier in East Germany in comparison with Argentina because the Government subsidised what could be bought. That way it could manage social unrest better. Here in Buenos Aires, no such tight control was in practice. The queues were for the banks. A lot of people were being paid daily in the Argentinian currency, australs and went immediately to a bank to turn it into US Dollars. This was the unofficial currency used by everyone who could. In crisis, or war conditions, it is the poorer families and pensioners who suffer most. No bank account, or access to one, meant sticking with money that depreciated rapidly.

What was it like being a short-term visitor? The first thing I noticed from a day-to-day point of view was that the price of my hotel breakfast changed each day, by a lot! The level of increase was different each day and I was never really sure if this was ok or not as the bill at the end of my stay would be converted to US Dollars. Not knowing the price of the same commodity each day is very unsettling, even for a person lucky enough to have reasonable expenses reimbursed.

Companies, where they could and where it was legal, traded in US Dollars. Of course, this was necessary to avoid a crisis turning into a disaster for the whole country. Three months before I arrived there had been riots in Rosario and Córdoba, the second and third largest cities and the government in Buenos Aires declared a state of emergency. Things were apparently under control about a month before I arrived. Our business here was an important part of my job at that time. However, I was beginning to think someone had it in for me.

It was in July. I had left the US in mid-summer; hot and humid. I arrived in mid-winter. It was grey, overcast and had been raining hard. It could have been England at any time of the year.

I had taken a straight forward taxi ride from the airport to the Intercontinental Hotel in the city. I went to the check-in desk and gave my name and reservation reference. The clerk gave me a cold stare. He excused himself and disappeared into the office at the back. I could hear several people talking excitedly. A new face popped around the doorway to look at me. More discussion and a completely new person, somewhat smarter dressed, came to my assistance.

"Is there something wrong with my reservation?"

The new person looked like he could be the manager. "No señor. Everything is ok"

"May I ask why my reservation caused your clerk to be so, startled?"

"I can assure you Señior Clutterbuck that everything is well with your reservation. It is your name that caused some, er, curiosity"

I refrained from my usual smart-arse remarks about my name and asked why.

"Well, sir, er, señor sir, we have had a little problem in the country. The head of one of our top car manufactures was kidnapped recently."

"Yes... and?"

"His last name was Clutterbuck."

"Oh, how dreadful for him," I said beginning to see why they were so interested in me when checking in. "Is it all settled and sorted out now?"

"Actually, yes it has, now." The manager was not looking as comfortable as he should, given that it had all been resolved. "His body was found last week. He had been shot in the head." I went to my room on the 7th Floor.

In my room was a message for me to meet the customer's Chief Financial Officer at a restaurant that night. A reservation had been made for 1:00 am! I was to meet David Lloyd. I had been travelling for about 20 hours and understandably it was the last thing I wanted. Normally, it would be the first thing. A meeting with the CFO would set up the whole trip and help me understand how to meet the sales objectives. Sales objectives in a hyper-inflation environment, with recent civil riots and a recent state of emergency, need a level of understanding not given out in any sales manual. The dinner didn't go as well anticipated.

The hotel concierge told me that the restaurant was very famous and was located in San Telmo, a well-regarded and oldest part of the city. The restaurant name meant 'The Wild Boar' in English. The concierge was very impressed that I had been invited by someone locally to eat at this prestigious place. So was I.

David Lloyd was a very distinguished, dignified and smart man. Although his suit was well worn, he was well presented. He greeted me with a clipped English accent.

Everything about him seemed English to me. The way he was courteous, his slight aloofness and willingness to see the humour in most things. However, I made two terrible mistakes.

Firstly, I asked David for a recommendation for the main course. I'd explained that due to travelling I only had an appetite for the main course. He ordered a starter and a main course for himself in effortless Spanish and said that since this was my first visit, I should try the wild boar. "Since this place is called 'The Wild Boar' and it is the house speciality you should try it, Paul." Wanting to curry favour with my new friend, I agreed and thanked him for his suggestion. He finished his starter and along came the main course. It was just a plate of meat. Wild Boar meat, rare. David asked me to begin and he sat still and watched. The taste and smell, was to be a similar experience eight years later when I was being encouraged to eat river rat in Tashkent. The taste is best described as 'gamey'. 'Strongly gamey'. The smell was pungent. The barely controlled impulse to wretch hit me immediately. He watched. I chewed. The gravy on the plate was a mixture of brown 'something' and blood. I cut small pieces of meat without looking at the plate and popped them in my mouth. I managed about half of the serving. As soon as he noticed I was going to keep it down, he started his own main course. His was also meat but something I had not recognised. He ate with gusto. I pushed my plate aside, out of my eye line. We talked about business and the economy and how our companies could do business. It was a good conversation. I felt like I was going to throw up at any time but didn't.

Second mistake. After a good business chat and a question from me about his main course — it was Llama — I asked him what part of England he came from.

"I'm Argentinian," he said sounding irritated and slightly offended. "But you must have been at school in England surely?"

"No. I was schooled here in Buenos Aires. I have never been to England."

"But you have a…" I stopped talking. It seemed best. An awkward pause.

He kindly restarted the conversation and shortly after he asked for the bill which was put in front of me. He just looked away until I produced US Dollars cash and paid up. He arranged a taxi for me and we agreed to meet towards the end of my trip. I had a few clarifying questions for my team the next day. I was completely exhausted, feeling sick and very confused. Only one of those feelings was unusual on my business trips. I don't normally feel sick.

Bruno

I had another message on returning to my hotel at 3:00 am. It was from my local team who said they would be along about 11:00 am to pick me up at the hotel. The desk clerk's gaze followed my walk from the entrance to the lift shaft. I guessed he knew I was 'The Clutterbuck'. I fell asleep and woke from the alarm clock at 10:00 am. I was ready and waiting in the reception area at 11:00 am.

At 11:30 am two young men walked in, looked around, agreed that my pale and tired-looking face must be the Englishman and came over.

"Señor Paul? Very nice to meet you. I am Bruno Espinola. This is our teammate Pedro." We continued with our small talk introductions and their polite inquiries about my travel and hotel arrangements. It was the normal, first meeting, business pleasantries which I've always found necessary to get started, but not sufficient by a long way for what we had to do together.

Bruno was tanned with longish black hair and smart, but old business clothes. He was about thirty years old. His manner was easy and he seemed to like the idea that an Englishman had taken the trouble to fly down and support his sales effort. He was surprised to find that I had flown from the US.

"US people don't like to come here. Too afraid of kidnapping. Haha." I laughed without giving away any of my recently gained knowledge about kidnapping in Argentina. We chatted a bit and I asked about them as people and their background.

Bruno had worked for our company for six years and was in a senior sales position. I asked what he did before that. He said he had to work in sales as the cattle ranch he owned didn't give him enough income. He had fifty gauchos employed on his ranch out in the Pampas. He had inherited it from his late father two years ago and was trying to organise it to make a profit. He went every weekend and his ambition was to make it a going concern within the next year. He told me one of his challenges were the ages of the gauchos. Some had been with his father for forty-five years and were worn out. He couldn't let them go because there were no young people coming through who wanted that kind of tough life in the modern world of the 1980s. His challenge was to try and hold the value of his cattle and farm and make it pay whilst operating in the chaos of hyperinflation. He talked at length about his background and upbringing. Sending himself to University against his father's wishes. His father had misunderstood what he had wanted to do with his education.

He told me, "Once I carry out my plan and make the cattle business profitable, I will then know that he would be proud of me. I always wanted him to be proud. The Gaucho life is one built on pride, prestige and dignity."

I found this really interesting as I had not known much about the country and its traditions and I told him so.

"We are so far from the rest of the world. Look at the map. We are at the bottom of a very long continent. We are more European in our culture, our architecture, our music, dance and sport than any other country in North and South America. We already have a well-developed and mature wine industry.

Chile is developing fast, but we are already established with our red wines. It takes a long time to travel here from just about anywhere else. Brazil is our nearest important neighbour but they have so many problems of their own, including inflation, that they don't look outwards. Paul, you coming here to help us with our business is highly significant and the customer will see that and see that we regard them as highly important."

At this fairly impassioned, articulate description of how he thought Argentina saw itself, I felt a complete fraud. I was there because I had business targets set and I needed Argentina to help meet my numbers. He must have known this of course but I was to feel this appreciation from many people during my visit. "Paul you are here until Tuesday which means I can show you a little of Buenos Aires, maybe Saturday because I do not need to return to my ranch until Saturday evening. For Sunday I recommend the market in San Telmo. I'm sure you'll pick up something to remember your trip."

He then introduced Pedro. He had been sitting listening. His English wasn't good but better, of course, than my

Spanish. Reading between the lines, Pedro was a sort of longtime school friend of Bruno who had got him the job in Buenos Aires. It seemed he was in thrall to Bruno.

Trying to understand

We drove to the office. I saw the queues for the banks. I noticed how polluting the single-decker buses were. Belching out thick, black diesel fumes. There were a lot of buses. Those that owned cars probably struggled to afford petrol.

We planned our sales calls and set ourselves sales objectives for the whole visit with at least a "Letter of Intent" signed with the customer before I left for home if not a full contract. Our first customer call was late afternoon with someone called Jorge.

Jorge was a lovely man, in his mid-fifties, who spoke no English. I did not speak Spanish. Eye contact and gestures were very friendly between us and every now and then he called out the name of an English football club or well-known English footballer. He tried using his best English accent that must have come from old black-and-white films but distorted because he didn't know where to place the emphasis on each syllable. He smiled a lot at me. I was pretty much a spectator in the whole meeting which lasted two hours. We had agreed something with Jorge and everyone was pleased with the meeting. From experience, I had learned to be attentive in meetings where I didn't know what the hell was going on. I was quite practised by that time in appearing to understand everything and to occasionally agree with something someone said when I detected that everyone in the meeting was already in agreement. The timing was key and staying alert for opportunities carried me through, even two hours of it. It was literally about understanding body language. The point was to participate in spirit and companionship without intellectually contributing. I knew Bruno was pretending that key ideas and actions were suggested by me as I heard "Señor Pablo" at critical points in the discussion — even though I didn't know what the ideas and actions were. Trust in your team is paramount.

We all shook hands and, as we were leaving, Jorge shouted after me with a huge grin, "Bibby Charleston!"*

I turned and called back "Diego Maradona." Jorge cheered, clenched his hands together high above his head and his huge smile displayed several missing teeth. I liked Jorge enormously.

Missing Laundry

It was about 7:30 in the evening when the team dropped me back at the hotel. I was starving. I got to my room and decided to order room service. I looked for the laundry I had put out that morning expecting it back in the room by now. The hotel had committed to having laundry back by 5:00 pm. No sign of the attractive laundry basket; it looked like a hamper and it had a clean white label on the top where you could write your name. I looked everywhere. No hamper. I called the reception and asked about it. They would call me back. They did five minutes later.

"Ah, Señior Clutterbuck. We have indeed delivered your laundry. It is written on the sheet "Entregado" by the laundry service staff."

"But I can assure you I have no laundry anywhere in my room. There must be some mistake."

"No mistake Señior. You must trust me. No mistake."

"Of course I trust you but I don't have it." I needed it for the next day, shirt, vest and underpants. I had extra socks. "Please check the number of the room it was 'Entregado'."

"Yes, sir. It was your room. Number 764."

"Ah, I think we have discovered the problem. My room is 762"

"Most sorry señior, please accept my humble apologies. And also ask you one favour. Señior Clutterbuck could you please go next door to number 764 and ask for your laundry. I am sure there will be no problem."

I knocked on number 764. As the door opened a tall, slim man with copious amounts of black, shiny, swept-back, heavily greased hair stood silently waiting for me to speak.

"Hola Señior. Siento interrumpir su velada. If possible, can we speak English? My Spanish is poor to non-existent as you will have just witnessed."

No response.

I ploughed on. "I believe my laundry has been delivered to your room by mistake. Is it possible that I may take it out of your way?"

"No. I have no your laundry señior."

"Oh, dear. The hotel has just told me that it was delivered to room 764 by mistake. I suppose you may not have noticed it. Maybe it's in your wardrobe?" As I said this, I saw the laundry hamper sitting on the floor just behind his left foot.

"Señor, I no have it?"

"Well, I think that might be it, just behind you on the floor." I doggedly stated pointing to the laundry basket behind his left foot! "No señior. This is for me, from the hotel. They have given me a gift I think"

"Well, it is a laundry basket. It has a shirt, underpants and vest in there. If you open it you'll see that that is what is in there. Besides, it has my name on it, written by me. In my handwriting."

Immediately he came towards me with his arms out wide. I needed my laundry but was not prepared to fight a fit-looking Argentinian for it.

"Señior! Señior!" he said very excitedly. "My name Clutterbuck. I am Juan Clutterbuck." He wrapped his arms around me in a strong hug. He kissed my cheeks twice. "We must be family. We must at least be friends."

Stupidly, we talked awkwardly for no more than a minute without ever trying to understand how we might be connected. He opened the basket and lo and behold my shirt, underpants and vest revealed themselves. He gave them to me, said a polite goodnight and shut his door.

I have often thought that this was a lost opportunity to understand how on earth so many Clutterbucks had come to Argentina. It is one of those things where it might be either really interesting, no discernible connection at all or a past family member roaming around South America following an incident or two in Europe during the 1940s. On balance, I think it was a missed opportunity.

A dash for the cash

The next two days were spent putting a sales proposal together for Jorge and his boss. We had a planned meeting on Monday and I was going to leave the following day, hopefully with a contract signed.

My arrangements for Saturday surrounded Bruno and Pedro showing me around. I had run out of Australs pretty quickly and I knew during the weekend I would need both local currency and US Dollars. Bruno said he knew how to get the best rate for buying Australs and arranged to do this on leaving the office before the weekend. I was to stay with him and do exactly what he says.

He drove us through backstreets in an old part of Buenos Aires and parked in a less than affluent looking car park next to a fairly scruffy ten-story apartment building. We took the stairs as there was no lift. The wooden balustrade staircase was wobbly, splintered and missing several pieces. We came to a door with no markings, numbers or names. Just a small wooden shutter at head height. Bruno knocked. We waited. He knocked again and the wooden shutter slid sideways and a pair of dark eyes peered at us. Bruno started talking in a style and tone I'd not seen before. Rapid exchange of Spanish between them ended with the shutter shut abruptly. Bruno held a hand up as if to say, 'wait'. We waited. Perhaps five minutes. The door opened and Bruno went in first. Pedro followed me. It was like a scene from an old black and white movie. Dim lighting, a table with money stacked in neat and equal piles. Heavy cigarette smoke. Yellow, nicotine-stained walls. Three men dressed in white shirts with waistcoats, black ties and arm gaiters to keep their shirt cuffs from restricting hand and money working together. The whole thing was a cliché. No one spoke but everyone was looking at me.

Bruno turned and said, "Two hundred US Dollars minimum. The best rate you will get anywhere. It's 40% better here than if you had walked into a bank in Buenos Aires today. OK?"

I wanted to ask how it all worked. How were they going to make money selling to me at 40% better than a bank?

Bruno quickly asked once more, "OK?" and looked at me without blinking.

"Yes. A very good deal," I said and I took the risk of

producing my wallet. Peeling off ten $20 notes and putting it back in my inside pocket in a fairly swift move. It made me want to laugh, but these chaps didn't look like they were in the mood for laughing. I took the australs without counting them.

Bruno shook their hands. Hugged them in turn. He took my arm and led me swiftly out the door, down the stairs and out to the car park.

"Please, Paul, you promise me you will not try to do this again. Certainly not on your own and please forget where this place is. I know these people and I know their families. It doesn't matter how I know them. I don't want to know any more than I do already. It's no good you asking what the set-up is because I don't want to know and you most certainly don't want to know anything either. By the way, it became difficult when they realised you were English. The Malvinas are still an emotional minefield. It would have been better had you not spoken at all."

We drove fast back to my hotel and made arrangements to meet in the morning.

The weekend — Rugby

It was a fairly damp day when Bruno and Pedro picked me up. We drove to the outskirts of the city to a sports ground. We were going to watch rugby. Bruno was known at this club but I can't remember its name. I felt the situation quite strange. Everything seemed very British. The rugby club, the sports ground and the weather. We enjoyed a bit of hospitality even though it was 11:00 am. Bruno was well known here. I was introduced to about half a dozen men before we reached the bar. They all were very welcoming and Bruno was turning into a very good host. Pedro said very little and, if I hadn't known better, I would have assumed he was Bruno's bodyguard and/or enforcer for reasons best known to them. We talked at the bar in English in a group of about ten people for maybe half an hour. The game started and we all watched it together. I was really struck how like England it was on this grey afternoon. Of course in July, here, it was mid-winter.

I said goodbye to my new friends in the car park as Bruno and Pedro drove me back into the city. I had offers to spend the evening with the rugby crowd in their bars and their homes. Their offers were actually quite touching and difficult to turn down. I can't remember why I did now and on reflection, it was another missed opportunity.

The weekend — Football Stadiums

We drove and eventually arrived at the Estadio de Nuñez, the national football team's home ground and home to possibly the most successful football club in the country — River Plate. It holds nearly 68,000 people and it's where the 1978 World Cup final was held between The Netherlands and Argentina. It's a formidable stadium. Bruno knew someone there and they let us into the empty stadium. Even empty it was intimidating, just the three of us. I remember clearly that famous football game and the wonderful sight of hundreds of thousands of pieces of ticker tape teeming and swirling around the whole stadium in celebration at the home team's win. It was a great experience to stand there in the most famous stadium in the country just looking around and walking on the pitch. Bruno wanted us to move on, there was another stadium he wanted me to see.

We had to drive south across Buenos Aires along busy, heavily polluted streets. I was glad to arrive at La Bombonera — home to Boca Juniors football club and apparently, I was told, as equally successful as River Plate. I realised immediately this was the team Bruno supported and made a mental note not to drop myself into discussions about football. I, of course, said that I felt La Bombonera was the better and more formidable stadium. He recanted the games he had seen here. How both he and his father had supported the team since childhood. Another man that Bruno knew showed us around and I felt honoured.

Back in the car, Bruno took a look at how I was dressed. He asked me to look inside the glove compartment where there were four neckties, all black. He asked that I put one on, nodded to Pedro and he put one aside for him. Again, we drove for some time until we came to an area which had seen better times. This next place was to be the most memorable of my trip to Argentina.

The weekend — Tango Dancers

We parked easily and walked into an old building similar in style to the old Victorian music halls of Britain. However, it was larger than those I'd seen in Britain and its exterior had a gently faded glory.

"Now we will see some Argentinian Tango!" he roared and gave me a big hug. "This is my favourite place in the whole of the city."

Someone Bruno knew ushered us into the large dance hall. Music was playing and there were about fifteen to twenty couples dancing. There was nobody sitting watching. Everyone in the hall was either dancing or playing in the dance band, except us. We sat in a ground floor box with a beautifully carved, rounded waist-high cubicle. The gold paint had faded, the orchestra pit hadn't been decorated in decades and although the wooden dance floor was in sound condition, it was scuffed and scarred. The lighting, what there was of it, was just bare, low wattage bulbs on their last legs. What we could see was faint, muted, softened.

"Just watch the dancers," Bruno encouraged me.

I watched mesmerised by the music, the beauty and the passion of the dance. I noticed that every one of the dancers must have been between the ages of sixty and eighty, maybe older. The men's jackets and trousers were heavily worn, sometimes darned and mostly ill-fitting but still they looked elegant.

They had either lost a lot of weight or had acquired someone else's clothes. Possibly both. Their shirt collars were frayed and turned up and sometimes curled over at the collar points. The women's dresses hung badly and were missing sequins here and there. However, it didn't matter at all. Each couple were staring into each other's eyes, almost glaring. The men had overwhelming lust in their eyes; their faces seemed as if they were etched in granite, staring unblinkingly at their dance partners. The women engaged their men with a look as if to ask "Are you really serious? Because I'll test your hunger for me, forever." The whole scene was breathtakingly poignant. The dancers, it was clear, were experts in Tango dancing and they showed so much love, lust, passion and devotion to each other in the authentic traditions of the Tango dance.

In between a dance number, Bruno leaned over and whispered to me. "You are wondering why I have brought you here?"

"Actually no, Bruno. It wasn't in my mind to wonder that question. But I do have some questions. May I?"

"Yes, of course," he said. Another number started and he pulled back. The dance finished a few minutes later.

I leaned forward and quietly spoke to Bruno. "The dancers seem to be only old people. Their clothes, and please don't take any nasty meaning from this, their clothes don't, er, seem right. Why is no one else here dancing also? Why does it seem so sad, yet so beautiful?"

He spoke quietly. "This is the only time in the week when it is free to enter and dance. These people have danced here all their lives. They have pensions that are worthless now. They live in houses that they can't maintain. They have nothing except their families who live close and this one-hour period is when they can dance. They have no money for the dance band who don't want money to play anyway. The dancers, however, want to maintain their dignity and composure. They bring vegetables or wash clothes as thanks. I brought you here to see these beautiful old people dancing so you know the true soul of Argentina. I come maybe once every six weeks and find fewer each time."

The band started on its' final number. As we left, I noticed briefly that Bruno had wept a little. He was very proud of his heritage and culture. I felt truly grateful to him for bringing me to this place and allowing me to be a spectator to the finest dancing I had ever seen.

The weekend — The market

Bruno and Pedro had dropped me at my hotel and we set a time of eight o'clock to meet on Monday morning at the office. He had given me a map and information of the Sunday market in San Telmo, a popular spot. I had the whole day to myself.

I had noticed the different styles of architecture in the city since I'd arrived. I say different because, although they were all European styles, I could see buildings in 17th, 18th or 19th century Paris, Madrid and London architecture. I had travelled throughout North and South America but Buenos Aires seems to have the mark of a truly European city. It was one of its several notable features. As I walked from my hotel to San Telmo, shortly before midday on Sunday, I easily imagined I was in one of those cities. The short walk was enjoyable and I felt really good about this business trip. It wasn't hard work, which is always a treat, and it felt as if we were going to get the business result, we needed. Now I wanted to explore on my own.

The large San Telmo market had three elements to it. Fruit and vegetables, local crafts and antiques. During the week, it was all housed inside a building with an Italian style facade. I'd learned that the market had originated in the late 1800s. It had been wonderfully preserved. On most Sundays, stalls were set up for anybody to claim space on the streets outside and sell whatever they wanted. What this meant at this moment, in a hyper-inflation economy, was that anyone who desperately needed money would literally sell the family silver to get through a few weeks. Only US Dollars were accepted for obvious reasons.

I thought I'd start with a coffee before browsing the market and stalls. Bruno had suggested a coffee shop/bar in the area. It was famous only because famous people visited. There were pictures of famous footballers (of course) but most of the photos were of local Argentinian celebrities whom I didn't know. There was one photo of Albert Einstein but the photo background didn't give its location so I supposed it was just there because the owner admired him. I noticed a small stage area and I was told that it was used two or three nights a week for exhibition Tango. Customers were given a cover charge no matter what was consumed. This café/bar was a beautiful place and it would fit in most European cities, especially Amsterdam.

Looking around the market, it took about an hour for something to catch my eye. I decided not to go into the building but to look outside at what the local people were selling to get by. There were three items that I was fascinated by but breezed by them and headed into the standard market building. In here it was a lot more formal and had most things you'd see in any town or city. Fruit and vegetables, most of which I recognised but a few I didn't. If Angie had been with me, we would have stopped and tried to talk to the stall owners to find out what they were, how to cook them and what you would serve with them. But it was just me, so I moved through. The arts and crafts were interesting however they were modern versions of old stuff and the pictures looked like the paint was still wet. I loved the market building and the local atmosphere. I could hear an accordion playing with violins and a singer but I couldn't see them.

Outside, I headed to my first stop. There, in the middle of a blanket, was an antique Argentinian Gaucho belt. It had an unusual buckle and silver and gold coins imbedded into well-worn leather. I fell in love with it. I went through my routine of explaining I could not speak Spanish and found that the man and woman selling their items could speak English reasonably well. They were probably in their 70s. They could have been dancing the Tango the evening before, in the empty dance hall.

"How old is this please señor?" I asked.

"It is ninety-one years old," the lady replied.

"It is beautiful. I love the buckle and coins and the leather looks ninety years old. Which I like. Have you owned it a long time?"

"My family has owned it for ninety-one years." The man looked at me for a reaction.

They must really need the money I thought. How much do I want it? How much am I prepared to haggle once they give me a price? Will I be able to look them in the eye as I try to beat them down? How much can I afford to spend on something that will just be looked at and never worn?

"How long have you been offering it for sale?" I asked without showing any signs except curiosity.

"About thirty minutes. This is our first time in the market on a Sunday. We are asking four hundred US Dollars."

Hmm, they really needed the money and they seemed unsure about the market price for any of their items or what to expect from potential customers who were just curious. This was a lot more than I could afford.

I looked at other items on the blanket. All of them looked like they were family heirlooms. There was something else that caught my eye. The lady saw my interest.

"Gaucho Bolas. The real name is Boleadora because there are three Bolas. I think you call them balls in English. If you have three balls it's called Boleadora. These are maybe only forty years old but were used a lot" she explained.

I've always been reasonably good at masking my ignorance, no matter what the subject. I wanted to pick them up and find out more about them. Each perfectly round ball was wrapped in leather and they were attached together with a long cord. But Gaucho Bolas could be what I was hoping they were not. Two were larger than the third but they were all potentially just that. Balls, from Gauchos. I stayed silent to see if my old trick would work here. Leave a gap in the conversation and the other person will fill it.

"Of course our family only ever used the best type of everything so these are stone, not wooden (thank God). They were used on our ranch. Our Gauchos were really expert at whirling them around their heads no more than three times before launching them at the legs of the cattle. When you have several hundred head of cattle these are the best way of bringing them down for branding quickly and then release. The American cowboys had a lot to learn from our Gauchos."

The old couple were looking at me with hungry eyes. I looked away and thanked them before moving on. The people on the streets had blankets and small tables displaying items they were desperate to sell. It seemed to me it was a buyers' market with sellers who didn't know how to price their products. How do you put a price on a much-loved family heirloom which is the last thing you want to sell? These may well be the last things they had to sell.

I found a wonderful set of antique silver cutlery. It was a complete set and hallmarked. It was intricately made and each piece seemed a masterpiece. I dived straight in.

"Is this from your family?" I asked without the ceremony of asking about speaking English.

"Señor, it is. It was from my Abuelo (grandfather). I need ninety dollars. Please señor."

I took seventy dollars from my wallet. I held it out and said, "Seventy and it's a deal." He took my money wrapped the silver cutlery in newspaper and handed it over without looking at me again. I walked away feeling guilty.

I walked up and down the stalls but kept a crafty eye on the lovely old couple with the belt and balls. I saw at least four people ask about the belt. There was much discussion between them but each time the potential customers walked away without buying. I stopped the last one of these further on down the street and asked about the belt. It seems the price being turned down was around one hundred and seventy dollars. He told me that actually, it would be a bargain at two hundred and twenty but he didn't have that amount of dollars. I went over to see them again.

"Ah Señor," I said, ignoring the lady who looked a harder person to deal with. "I am pleased to see you still have your Bolas!" This attempt at humour was pathetic and Angie would have kicked me hard. But I didn't want them to see I was really interested in the belt.

"Si Señor, we also have the Gaucho belt." They had sold one or two items since I had been talking to them last but their blanket still looked quite full.

"Would you consider two hundred dollars for the belt?" They looked at each other and, unfortunately for them, seemed to quickly agree. "To include the Boleadora."

I had to hold my nerve as they winced. I took out two hundred dollars and showed it to them. Once they saw the cash the deal was done. What a completely nasty person I am. Without looking at me again they wrapped the belt and balls separately in newspaper, handed them to me and took my cash. No further words were spoken, except for me thanking them. I tried to shake their hands which didn't happen. I have never, ever felt as bad about buying something. As much money as they were, these items would fetch far more outside of Argentina than inside. I have never sold them. How could I? They are now part of my family heirloom. I still feel guilty.

Very guilty. This is how market forces should work normally, except that normally no one really feels guilty. I did.

The closing

That Sunday evening, I thought about the next day and the sales proposal we were going to make to Jorge — my new friend who shouts out English footballers' names. Something had caught my attention when we were planning the proposal on Friday. Every piece of equipment provided by our company was rented. I had briefly gone through the computer printout (yes, the old style green and white striped paper) which listed everything we charged monthly in dollars. I'd brought the listing back to the hotel. That evening I went through it again. I noticed Keypunch machines on the listing. Punch cards? In 1989? You must be joking. Yes, there they were, three machines. Monthly rental charges. I checked the computer supplies charges and saw no punch cards sold in the last six months. They weren't using them and, as they had not returned them, they were still being charged. This is something positive we can do for them I thought.

Monday morning, the proposal was ready. This was to be the biggest sales proposal of the year to this customer. Pedro had worked all Sunday to get it ready for us and Bruno hugged and kissed him on both cheeks by way of thanks. Pedro was almost blushing. I shook his hand, grateful that I was English and that we didn't do that sort of thing where I came from.

"What obstacles might we have to get this proposal agreed by close of business today?" I asked.

"Señor Pablo, it is traditional to make sure the customer has something they can show inside their company that they won in negotiations. A sort of bravado, courage or as we say 'Valentía'. The prices are standard. Rental is the normal way of business in Argentina today so there is not much we can really give them." Bruno looked pensive.

I spoke immediately "I have an idea. I noticed three Keypunch machines still on our monthly rental charges. How about we declare them owned by the customer. After all, they will have paid more than enough rental by now to have bought them outright. We can then buy back the Keypunch machines for a 'computer museum' we are thinking of establishing. Exactly what we would pay them to buy them back is up to you but it seems everyone wins, if we pay them the total amount we've charged them, since they became redundant. We save face, they save face and it looks like we have something to give them. What do say?"

A huge smile lit up Bruno's face. He ignored the mysterious 'computer museum' idea. Nobody was looking to set that up but it was a good distraction. Off we went to meet Jorge.

"Bibby Moors!"[6] Jorge greeted me with the same semi-toothless grin.

I could see from the colour of his teeth he was a smoker as well. After the normal time taken for handshaking and enquires about the weekend between Jorge, Bruno and Pedro we sat down and went through our new sales proposal. Jorge looked up at the end and expected the 'bravado' item. Bruno took him through the story of the keypunch machines. I've been in enough meetings held in languages I don't understand to get a sense of what was being said and how the story was being told (or sold in this case). Jorge punched the air. He could see how this was going to make him look good without any of the detail about paying for redundant keypunch

---

[6] *Actually Bobby Moore, West Ham United, England and World Cup winner.*

machines. Then his expression changed. I could tell he was thinking in slow motion. He did this while trying to disguise the troubled shadow that plagued his expression. I guessed what was going on. Later, after I had returned to the USA, I learned why he felt so awkward. My instincts were about right.

The contract was put together and agreed with Jorge and his boss. The next day Pedro would be getting it all printed and signed by all those who had to, in both companies. We left the office with Jorge and headed to a bar close by. This was my last night there and Bruno wanted to mark the occasion. We had a small drink, an aperitif I suppose, but it came from a bottle the colour and name I had not seen before. If I'd had this drink the first night then it would definitely have masked the taste and smell of the wild boar. It was that distinct. We were all together well into the evening. Towards the end, Bruno stood up, climbed on the table and told me that I was an honorary Gaucho and could have a job on his ranch at any time. He then told me it is customary for the ranch owner to sing a song in honour of the new recruit. He sang at the top of his voice a moving and slow ballad style song. Towards the end of the song, tears were moving down his face. The whole bar was silent while he sang. He stopped to generous applause. He then said I was now obliged to return a song to the bar. The bar fell silent as I stood up wondering what to sing. Then it came naturally, as if from a predetermined source. My friend, Pat Hosey from Wilmington, Delaware, had taught me a new Limerick just days before I had left for Argentina. I stood and belted out;

"An Argentinian Gaucho, named Bruno,
said there is one thing I do know,
A woman is fine,

A man divine,
but a Llama is numero uno."

I sat down in silence. I saw Pedro staring at me which made me uncomfortable, to say the least. Jorge was bewildered as he did not understand a word. The people in the bar didn't move a muscle. Bruno came over to me laughing his head off and gave me a man hug. Everyone relaxed and those that had understood me had started to laugh too. Bruno asked me to write it down; he was going to use it again he said. They said goodbye and thanked me for coming south to help them. I rode to the hotel in a taxi with a warm heart and a lot of affection for all the people I had met.

My wet departure

It rained hard the next morning on the way to the airport. The taxi driver was friendly enough. He spoke on the phone as we were about halfway to the airport. We were stopped on the approach road by two Police. It was raining hard. A large policeman asked me to get out of the car. My raincoat was packed in a suitcase. I wasn't expecting to be exposed to the elements. He had cover from a canvas tent arrangement. He wanted to see my passport and asked me in English to show him how many US Dollars I was taking out of the country. The market had seen off most of it so I showed him the forty dollars I still had. He told me the Buenos Aires Police exit fee was exactly forty US Dollars. I handed over the money, he gave me my passport back and ushered me back into the car. The driver was not impressed with the rainwater making the passenger seat in the back soaking wet. The rain was running from my head down the back of my neck. I noticed the driver seemed to know the Policeman.

I was able to dry off a little in the Pan Am lounge and boarded the plane uneventfully. About an hour into the flight the man next to me knocked a whole glass of water onto my seat while I was in the toilet. The seat was soaking. The best the cabin staff could do was put paper towels, lots of them on the seat to soak up the wet. The plane was full and it was a ten-and-a-half-hour flight. They were running out of paper towels they could spare for my seat. I was tired and sat down when the last possible towel had been used. An improvement but damp, really damp. With the air-conditioning roaring, I felt cold, really cold.

I arrived in the US to ninety degrees Fahrenheit (thirty-two Celsius). I had shivered most of a truly unpleasant journey. As I stood in the car hire parking area, with the hot sun on my back, I daren't look to see if steam was rising from my rear end.

It was good to be home from a truly unforgettable business trip. I was looking forward to seeing my family and Pat, my limerick source, and the rest of the USA team of Bill, Tony and Geoff.

We over-achieved our sales targets for 1989 in Argentina.

As ever,

Paul

PS: The reason Jorge had a worried look on his face as we were completing the deal was the realisation that someone had sent the keypunch machines to a scrap yard a few years before. He need not have worried, no one ever asked about them, as far as I know, in either company.

PPS: I didn't meet David Lloyd, my 1:00 am dinner date,

again. He had enjoyed his free Llama meal.

PPS: Bruno left his job the following year to run his ranch and manage his Gauchos. Pedro joined him.

PPPS: Jorge left his job two years after my visit.

New Yorkers on a hot sunny day on Coney Island

14. Coney Island Deposits
New York

Dear Brendan,

Unlike a lot of businesses in other industries, in my opinion, banks are not interesting per se. Whether they sell insurance, banking, savings, loans or investments, the firms themselves and their products, although vital, are by and large boring. Never one to shirk a challenge, I have come across a bank worthy of a letter to you.

This story has been put together because I think you would have liked it. It involves an entrepreneur, a mini banking discrepancy and some of the good people of Coney Island, Brooklyn, New York. I have written it as best I could, given the fading memory of my friend, Kevin La Croix, who told me most of it. I only went to Coney Island once. It was winter and it was closed.

A Bank in the dog eat hotdog world

The Bank of Coney Island building was built c.1923 on West 12th Street, just south of Surf Avenue. The bank was designed by Holmes & Winslow, architects that specialised in bank design. In short, it was a beautiful building of its type and for that era.

The bank was opened in 1909 by local businessmen to serve and strengthen the immediate area of Coney Island. They had noticed that other banks, only a few miles away and in less populated areas, had been extremely successful. It was expected that this bank, which was "purely of local concern and will draw its support entirely from the islanders," would also be extremely successful.

The bank's first president and primary petitioner to New York State for the bank's formation was Stephen A. Jackman. Besides banking, he was an early developer of roller coasters and amusement rides. He and his brother arrived in Coney Island in 1890, and over the years, they developed several early Coney Island roller-coasters and rides, including the Blue Slide, the Victoria Slide, Jackman's Thriller, Whirlwind Ride, and Shooting the Rapids. Among early founders of the Bank of Coney Island were other well-known Coney Island land and amusement owners. These included Frederick

Henderson of Henderson's Hall; Charles Feltman of Feltman's beer garden (where the hotdog was invented); Henry Grashorn of the Grashorn hardware store; and William J. Ward, owner of much of the land along Jones Walk, proprietor of Ward's baths and other amusements, and developer of Coney Island's Half Moon Hotel. Ward eventually became president of the Bank of Coney Island, serving for two decades. The bank had an interesting diversity of founders, to say the least.

It was independent until 1927 when it was acquired by the National American Company and then sold to the Brooklyn Trust Company in early 1928. It was very successful, particularly in the summer months when deposits swelled. In the 'dog eat dog' world of banking it is evident that banks eat other banks and, in this case, in 1950, the bank was swallowed whole by the Manufacturers Trust Company, which was later renamed the Manufacturers Hanover Trust Company in the 1960s. The Bank of Coney Island building continued to be a branch of the Manufacturers Hanover Trust until about 1990. I'll tell you what happened then, later in my letter.

Banking in those days

Kevin describes banking in those days as being a 3-6-3 business. Banks borrowed money at 3%, charged 6% for loans and the manager was on the golf course by 3 pm. If you made an appointment to see the manager, knocked on his door (yes, it was always a man) the conversation might go like this.

"Good morning, what can I do for you?" — manager "How do I stand for a mortgage?" — potential customer "You don't. You kneel." — manager.

The principal measure of banking in those days was NIM — Net Interest Margin with income from fees regarded as trivial (the reverse is true today). But then there was the Bank of Coney Island (BoCI). When my friend Kevin arrived at the bank, he found the manager to be bright, charming and an entrepreneur. When looking at the accounts he noticed deposit fees soared during the four summer months and the bank made more in fee income than any other retail branch in Manufacturers Hanover Trust, by a mile. He was to learn why by using the best methods available to mankind. Kevin watched carefully and knew when to ask the right question, to the right people.

Seymour (a.k.a. Maxi)

Seymour Maximilian Hyram Gaslowitz was called Maxi by his customers. He was called many other things growing up in Brooklyn, New York. His parents had always thought that he would stand out if they gave him three initials before anyone got to his last name. However, he stood out for many other reasons.

For a start, Maxi was very bright. He was quick on the uptake. He sensed things around him that took others a lot longer to notice. He assessed people with whom he came into contact much quicker than anyone else. He worked hard at school to try and rise above those who tried to put him down. Almost everyone tried to put him down: his classmates; some of his teachers; and his neighbours. He made them all feel uncomfortable. He just wasn't like them.

Maxi didn't play sport. He liked to read; anything and everything. He loved numbers. Very early on it was adding and subtracting. Then he understood multiplying and dividing. He moved on rapidly in the fields of maths, science and literature leaving others of his age way behind. He developed an educated, broad and inquisitive mind. Very dangerous for a boy growing up in Brooklyn, in the 1950s. He was very lucky by finding two teachers to help him grow at his own pace in maths and literature. Science was regarded as elitist and not something a Brooklyn boy needed to worry about.

Maxi was liked by girls as he grew up and he preferred to be with them when no one else wanted him around. He preferred what they played with, what interested them and what they talked about. He remained single all his life. Maxi became a well-loved and well-known Jewish member of the Coney Island community.

Maxi joined the Bank of Coney Island from school and worked his way up. He was the Branch Manager when my friend Kevin was assigned by his employer to 'learn banking' with a loyal customer, Manufacturers Hanover Trust. He spent a few weeks as a Personal Assistant to Maxi in 1969.

Coney Island

For most of the twentieth century, Coney Island was the summer playground for New Yorkers. It is well known for its large beach and fun-fair attractions. As Blackpool is to the English, Coney Island was to New Yorkers. It was, and is, well served by roads, buses and trains. During hot and humid summers, it was a blessing for the city dwellers to go to the beach and feel the sea breeze. In the days that Maxi was branch manager, Coney Island was a residential, beach community that was heavily Jewish. A perfect match for what was to transpire.

Making money from modesty

The Bank of Coney Island was across the street from a large public beach. The beach was equipped with public changing booths so people could change into their bathing suits and then back to street clothes after a day at the shore.

However, the modest Jewish women of the neighbourhood did not think it was proper to use the booths. Maxi being a good Jewish member of the community, a hit with the ladies and bright as a button, had a solution. A customer could rent a safe deposit box by the day, change clothes in the vault, enjoy the beach and protect their modesty.

So, every day, during the summer months, ladies would enter the bank with their bathing suit in a paper bag, and be escorted to the vault by a female teller. They would change clothes in private, leave their street clothing in the safe deposit box and enjoy the beach. In the afternoon the process would be reversed. The female tellers would take turns sweeping up the sand from the floor of the vault.

When most banks were charging $5.00 a year for a safe deposit box, Maxi was getting $0.75 cents each day for four months. The branch had more deposit boxes per square foot than any branch in New York. And every summer all of these new savings accounts would be opened so the account holders could have access to a safe deposit box and protect their modesty.

As far as Kevin could tell, the manager was not on the golf course (or the beach) every day at 3:00 pm. He could be found, however, offering iced tea, lemonade or other light refreshments as the deposit account customers returned from the cool breezes just as the branch went through their daily 'closing out' procedures.

I can't imagine that today the financial authorities in the USA — Federal Deposit Insurance Corporation (FDIC), Comptroller of the Currency, Financial Action Task Force (FATF), the Federal Reserve Bank, the Department of the

Treasury and the FBI — allowing the Bank of Coney Island to provide this invaluable community service to Carmel, Esther, Miriam, and Sadie.

Entrepreneurial life evolves

The parent bank closed the branch in 1990. Then, in the 1990s, the building was used as the International Circus Museum, which exhibited curiosities and occasional live acts and was operated by Bobby Reynolds. Bobby Reynolds was known then as the World's Greatest Showman, a modern-day Barnum. Bobby grew up working at Coney Island as a shoeshine boy, selling horn nuts, and learning magic until he got a job at Hubert's Museum with Professor Heckler's trained flea circus. He worked night clubs, cabarets, vaudeville, variety and pretty much every venue and performance opportunity in the United States. Bobby was once featured on the cover of Weekly World News with his authentic two-headed baby, Ronnie and Donnie. He ran seven shows at once, was the president of the Showman's Association and Show Folks of America, sold pens and developed a healthy addiction to cheesecake.

And finally...

UPDATE August 14, 2010: (Thanks to the website 'amusingthezillion.com) "We're sorry to report the demolition permit for the bank building was issued yesterday — Friday the 13th. It was no surprise because on Wednesday the sidewalks around the Thor-owned building were being dug up to disconnect sewer and water lines in preparation. How inexpressibly sad to see the potential here and what will be gone forever in a matter of days. Don't bother calling the DOB to complain either. It's final! According to the permit: 'This job is not subject to the Department's Development Challenge Process. For any issues, please contact the relevant borough office.' Yeah, we have an issue."

No trace left. Nothing.

As ever,

Paul

PS: I don't know what happened to Maxi or the good and modest bathing ladies of Coney Island, greater Brooklyn and New York City.

(*My thanks to my good friend Kevin La Croix for telling me this story.*)

15. Yasser and me
Jordan

Dear Brendan,

In 2003 I said yes to a visit to a bank in Jordan. Not the bank on the river Jordan, but a bank which mainly lent money to the property market. The visit was to be full of surprises.

A previous work colleague, Ewan, called me, told me what was needed, told me it was a visit in which only expenses, reasonably incurred, would be covered and asked if I was interested. "Oh, and it's only three days and it's in Amman, Jordan." I was just about to say no thanks when he slipped in,

"Oh, and on day two we have a holiday and the customer would like to provide a car, driver and guide to take us to Petra. You may have heard of it. It's quite well known. It's a World Heritage Site." I agreed, without hesitation. Ewan knew me quite well.

The task was straight forward. A few interviews, review marketplace information and important banking performance, assess the bank's position against competition and report to the Chairman on the third day. Ewan had brought along much of the information needed beforehand. I wanted to know from Ewan why we were asked; what was the point of this visit? His view, and also that of the bank. I felt his answer was a bit thin on both points but why look a gift horse in the mouth. I was going to visit Petra all expenses paid!

Petra

The journey to Jordan and the Amman hotel were not noteworthy. On day one, I enjoyed being a business detective again. It was a very positive customer and a positive analysis was put together. All we had to do was review it with the Chairman before leaving on day three, following our excursion to Petra.

Ewan and I were up early on day two. It was about a three-and half-hour car journey to Petra from Amman so we needed to get going. Very soon we were in flat, desert terrain. There was very little traffic in either direction. Our driver, Zaid, told us not to worry, he had made this journey more than a hundred times. I had my doubts as he looked about nine years old.

Our guide, Omar, explained that since 9/11 almost no American and very few European tourists had visited Petra. He told us that a lot of tourism workers had government-funded jobs so they personally hadn't suffered. It was those who were "unofficial" tourism workers that had been hit badly. The unofficial workers were the poor of the area who had roadside, walkway and family stalls in or along the way to the archaeological site.

Driving through a sandstorm, but with almost no one to swerve to avoid on the road, we arrived to be greeted by no one. The coach park was empty. The Mövenpick hotel car park was empty. Our car pulled up and six guides remained seated, playing what looked like backgammon. The youngest looked up at us, saw we had a guide and focused again on the game at hand.

We set out by walking through a valley known as Bad as-Siq for about half a mile. This gritty, desert track takes you passed huge Nabatean funerary blocks that stand as sentinels at the entrance to the ancient city. What follows is known as the "Siq." The name, in rough translation, means "Shaft." The name is very apt. It is an impressive 80 metres high, mile-long, red sandstone canyon that leads you into Petra. Jagged cracks and peaks, mixed with multiple hues of red sandstone come together to make this a formidable introduction to this ancient city.

Omar was very good at his job. He explained, at length, about the Nabatean civilisation and its control over world trade through its domination of east to west trade routes. It was 2,600 years ago that they carved Petra out of sandstone.

Omar trying to slow us down

Omar continued effortlessly, almost without stopping for breath and with great detail. He told us he was so happy that day because he hadn't worked for about seven months. No tourists. We kept walking while he kept talking. He really knew his subject but I'm afraid my brain was full after 15 mins! Both Ewan and I were trying to set a quicker pace, but Omar stopped every now and then, to slow us down. This would mean he could keep talking for longer.

The canyon floor was flat, dry as a bone and sloped downwards. It was so narrow at times that only one person could pass through. I was feeling dizzy and our verbose guide's voice was becoming hypnotic. Over the space of the mile and a half since setting out, Omar had talked non-stop. I thought I saw blood oozing from Ewan's ears but it was just me hallucinating. It was a challenging walk. Just the four of us. We didn't see anyone else during the whole journey. Then we were at the end of the roofless tunnel.

Our first view of the Treasury, Petra

Before us was a magnificent sight: the first glimpse of the Treasury building through the steep-sided slit of a pass.

Then we were out into the open and the whole historic city was on view.

I know you will have seen pictures of the very impressive Treasury building. It's basically a huge facade carved meticulously into the side of the rock face and in a sheltered part of a valley (Wadi al-Jarra). Its position has provided protection from wind, rain and direct sunlight (except briefly morning and evening) allowing the facade to retain its crisp and clean-cut craftsmanship. It hasn't, however, escaped damage from various iconoclasts over many years. The total area against the side of the cliff is about forty metres by thirty metres. Enormous. If you watched the film Indiana Jones and the Last Crusade you will certainly know the image. Unfortunately, it is essentially just a facade. Inside there's only a dull, blank square chamber, with smaller rooms opening from it. One of the few questions I asked Omar made him pause for breath.

"Omar, why is it called the Treasury?"

He didn't know. He was briefly quiet.

"Nobody seems to know," he said and went quiet again.

Nobody seems to have even made something up. I would. The name obviously implied that the city kept its treasures, money or valuables inside. But it is tiny and there are rumours that it was a Royal Tomb which would make sense calling it the Treasury in that case.

The site is massive. It deserves two or three days to explore with a guide who doesn't drench the visitor with information at a savagely fierce speed and drowning volume. Omar was, without question, highly knowledgeable but we were victims of his lack of recent practice.

Meeting Yasser

I suggested to Ewan we split up and went at our own pace through the site and agreed to meet back at the Treasury in two hours. It was fifty-fifty which one of us Omar would stick to. I was the one in luck - he picked Ewan.

I could write about the history of the whole site, but I feel you'd want to know more about the people I found there. For thousands of years, people have slept inside the caves that you can see in Petra's lunar-like landscape. The Jordanian government relocated its cave dwellers to a nearby village two kilometres away thirty years previously in an attempt to preserve Petra. It became a UNESCO World Heritage Site a little after that.

So, no tourists, no cave dwellers, the site should be empty. It pretty much was, apart from us, two camels and one (paid to be there) sentry dressed in the traditional Jordanian Royal Guard uniform, with rifle and bullets on display. I guessed the camels were for tourists to take a ride and it was clear they wouldn't be worked hard that day, if at all.

I headed away from the Treasury on my own and along the short valley with high cliffs on either side. It was a spectacular place to be wandering by myself. Then I spotted a small boy a few hundred yards away. He was standing staring at me. He was almost invisible as he seemed to merge into the landscape. He saw me coming towards him slowly, smiling and waving. He ran away from me and into a cave. Less than a minute he reappeared with an old, bent, wooden box. He then bent down picked up some rocks, put them in the box and walked towards me. His face was dirty with dry mud, his hair was dusty.

"Lo mister," he said and offered me a rock. "One dollar."

Instinctively, I wanted to laugh but didn't. To me, this was such a profound representation of dignity when in a state of poverty. Begging was not for him. He wanted to sell me something and the only products available were the rocks on the ground. I gave him a US dollar and he gave me a rock. He then said, "For your wife," and he offered me another rock. I gave him a dollar and he gave me another rock. He had three left in his tray. I gave him three dollars and took the remaining rocks. His face was a picture, so I took his photograph. It's at the top of this letter.

"My name is Paul. What is your name?"

"Yasser," he said.

Yasser lived somewhere here

I thanked him and set off to explore. Yasser followed me for the rest of the two hours until I returned to our meeting place at the Treasury. He disappeared before anyone else saw him.

I mentioned Yasser to Omar who looked very uncomfortable. He told me that it was impossible that I had met anyone from the caves because it was forbidden for anyone to live there. He went on about the cave-dwelling tradition of the Bedul tribe and that Bedouins were allowed to work and sell items in Petra but not live there. Zaid, our driver, whispered to me that indeed there were Bedouins living in the caves but no one wanted to recognise it. It was forbidden. They were supposed to be invisible.

Ewan looked word weary. He walked ahead of the three of us, Omar, Zaid and me and I think he wanted to rest his ears. The return journey through the mile-long, narrow canyon was quite hard. I hadn't really noticed the slope going downwards on the way into Petra but after trudging around for two hours, climbing up and down rocks, paths and caves, it was exhausting. As I walked, Omar told me stories of people drowning in the gorge. It was hard to believe when everywhere I looked was bone dry and dusty. However there have been flash floods every now and then where people have been swept down the narrow gorge, some died.

We got back to the car and Ewan got in the front seat, next to Zaid, leaving me to rub shoulders in the back seat with Omar for the three- and half-hour trip back to Amman. Ewan gave me a wry smile, closed his eyes and slept peacefully all the way back. I was entertained by the highly knowledgeable but over-excited Omar all the way back. I'm sure he accidentally, on purpose, nudged me each time my eyes started to close and my head was dropping forward. It was a long, long ride back.

The other photographs

The third day was report day. We were asked to go straight into the Chairman's office. I looked into his cold, black eyes. I felt the firm, strong handshake. I noticed his expensive clothes. I smelt a strong blend of soap, coffee and aftershave. He was not to be trifled with and I was immediately aware of giving the man what he wanted; a glowing report with areas for a slight improvement. Ewan told me he was going to use it to boost the bank's, and his, prestige. So, now I knew what it was all about. Also, he wanted to sack someone and the areas for improvement would support this in his mind. He was very charming once he had heard what we had to say in the report and he guided us to sit on sofas and armchairs he had installed in the non-business end of the office. He pressed a button on his desk and a young boy, he looked about five years old, came in wearing a smart uniform and poured us mint tea.

The Chairman asked, "So, my good friends, what did you think of your day return to Petra?"

"Firstly, I want to thank you for your generosity in providing a car, driver and guide for our day," Ewan said. "The car was very comfortable and your driver Zaid, excellent. But I have to say that we could not have wished for a better guide than Omar. My colleague Paul was particularly impressed."

"Do you want to say something Paul?" the Chairman asked.

"I spent a little time wandering alone and met a Bedouin boy who sold me some rocks. They were a dollar each. He let me take his picture. I have it on my camera. Here it is. His name is Yasser." I showed him the photograph.

"Delightful, I'm sure," he said. "Now, I'd like to show you some photographs." He turned in his swivel Chairmans chair, opened doors to a cabinet and there were three photos of him kissing and hugging a very famous figure of the twentieth century. "This is my friend Yasser and me.[7] We grew up together."

As ever,
Paul.

---

[7] *Mohammed Yasser Abdel Rahman Abdel Raouf Arafat al-Qudwa al- Husseini, popularly known as Yasser Arafat.*

PS: I still have the five rocks, from my Yasser, on the mantlepiece at home.

Angie with a Sadhu in the pink city of Jaipur

16. Jail is a safer place
India

Dear Brendan,

Unlike some places I've visited, India lived up to both its positive cultural richness and its gritty reputation.

Angie was a little more reticent but we had both always liked the idea of a trip to India. It was 2004 and after flying into Delhi, the plan was to travel by train throughout Rajasthan, for a week. Following that, we were to fly to the holiest of Hindu and Jain cities and a major place of pilgrimage, Varanasi, returning to Delhi for the last three nights.

The "Palace on Wheels" train was billed as a luxury, ex-Maharaja accommodation on which we would eat most meals in specially equipped carriages. The train's carriages weren't used by the Indian Railways following independence in 1947 because they were of high value but high maintenance cost with very traditional interiors. The priority in India at that time was to operate trains capable of mass passenger transit. The train was basically mothballed until 1982 when it restarted as a regular tourist experience.

The wine box incident

We shared our carriage, or saloon as it was called, with two other couples. One couple, John and Mary from Detroit, worked for car manufacturers. The other couple were from Maryland, Felix and Joan. Felix was one of the few French wine importers to the USA and clearly a rich man. Wine is still regarded as a type of "luxury" beverage in many areas of the USA. Joan was an academic and very well read. The six of us were served throughout the week solely by two 'Palace on Wheels' personal staff, Raam and Ali. They were available to us 24 hours a day. Raam seemed to be more senior than Ali but there didn't appear to be seniority in their roles or duties. The train comprised 14 saloons each having two staff, plus 2 restaurant saloons.

The idea of the journey was to travel by night between cities or interesting places throughout Rajasthan so that we could use daytime at our stops. From Delhi, we stopped in Jaipur, Jodhpur, Udaipur, Jaisalmer, Agra (Taj Mahal),

Ranthambhore tiger reserve and a beautiful bird sanctuary amongst other notable places. It sounded great and it was.

The reality of Maharaja 19th/20th century luxury and 21st century expectations of luxury didn't quite match. As lovely as our saloon was, comfortable it wasn't. The toilets needed updating first to 20th century standards and then careful consideration could be given to luxury for the 21st century. However, expectations do need to be reset according to where you are in the world. The bathroom facilities were about the same size and cleanliness as a facility on a regular train in Britain. In other words, not very big and not as spotless as needed for seven straight days.

Our dedicated saloon staff, Raam and Ali, were great. I got to know Raam better. He had a very endearing personality, partly because he used to sway his head profusely side-to-side in almost every situation. It is a mannerism you often see in India and Sri Lanka. A sort of sideways nod. To westerners, it seems odd. In this part of the world it is a way of communicating without speaking. I'd ask him a question and he'd sway his head in answer. The answer might be yes, no or maybe. He visibly weighed up the conversation. His facial expression would give his final answer. I once had a complete conversation with him where he only swayed his head and somehow, I knew what he was saying. Every morning he would, almost imperceptibly, knock on our door at exactly the same time and produce a breakfast menu. The same breakfast menu each day. I would choose the same breakfast, cornflakes I think, followed by a chicken sausage and scrambled eggs. Each time I gave him my order, he would shout with childlike glee,

"Yes, why not sir! GO FOR IT."

Every day the same routine. The way he spoke was as if Raam was indicating I was taking a risk. That is, gambling with my breakfast in an exciting way. One day I asked if it were possible to have porridge instead of cornflakes. It completely threw him. He immediately had a pleading look on his face. I gave in and ordered my routine breakfast. You know, the really risky breakfast. I think it was the only one he was allowed to provide.

When we first arrived at the train, we handed Raam and Ali, all baggage and personal effects so that they could prepare our cabin (bedroom and bathroom). Among the personal items I gave him was a three-litre white wine box which we had brought from England. We'd learnt when travelling in places to take a wine box with us. He took the box and looked puzzled.

"Raam, this is a wine box. Would you please put it in a refrigerator to keep it cool? We were hoping to have it served early evening, before dinner, and perhaps also after. Would this be ok with you?"

He still looked puzzled but this time more worried. He swayed his head from side-to-side and then took care of all of our luggage.

That evening, about an hour before dinner, I pressed a button which I was told would buzz Raam and Ali where they had a small compartment with a kitchen and beds. This is where they would prepare snack food and drink for the guests and rest or sleep. It was at the end of the saloon and we would walk past it to go to lunch or dinner. Raam came almost immediately.

"Yes, Mister Paul," he swayed his head.

"Good evening, Raam. Would it be possible for Angela

and I have to have a glass of wine before dinner?" My request got a head sway in reply.

He was gone maybe twenty minutes. If he left it longer, we would be going to the restaurant car so I decided to slip along to their compartment which contained the fridge. To my surprise, I saw Raam and Ali fairly frantically trying to work out how to get the wine out of the box. I could see what was happening; they didn't know what to do and were afraid of damaging the box.

"Ah, yes, Raam. This is a very new way of pouring wine. Please let me have the honour of showing you and Ali how this works."

I opened the tab at the bottom, pulled out the pouring spout, took off the plastic seal, asked for the glasses and then showed them how to pour. They were goggle-eyed. I then asked them to pop the box back in the fridge to keep it cool and headed back to our cabin.

We went to dinner, passing Raam and Ali's compartment. The sliding door was shut. We had a good meal and made our way back to our cabin. As we approached Raam and Ali's door we saw two turbaned men in the corridor peering into their compartment. They looked nervous as they saw us approaching. I looked around the door to see Raam looking up at the box, from a kneeling position, as Ali held it above his head. Raam immediately swayed his head in greeting. Raam performs curiosity, not embarrassment, really well. He had a frown and an almost pleading look in his eyes. His head swaying from side-to-side.

"Mister Paul. How does it work?"

"Vacuum, Raam."

It was the best answer I could think of because I hadn't

really thought about it before. There is so much I take for granted without understanding how things worked I realised.

Five minutes later, I passed Raam and Ali's compartment once more to find seven staff gathered in the passageway or squeezed through their doorway. In the dim, soft light I saw Raam demonstrating the wine box. He had joy in his eyes and a broad smile. He was showing-off to his friends. The glass he was squirting my wine into was almost full.

I asked, "Would it be possible to pour another glass for Misses Angela, please, Raam?"

He did so with a sense of pride, in front of his friends and colleagues.

Raam and Ali spent seven months of each year on the train without a break. The remaining five months were spent with their families. Raam had done this for twenty years, Ali just fourteen. They appeared very happy and proud of their work. I have often thought of them and how rare it is to find people so enthusiastic and proud of their existence.

The train journey

It was an adventure. It was everything I had hoped for in our first visit to India. Great expanses of inhabited land and uninhabitable desert. Friendly, easy-going people. The sound of our train's whistle sounding deep into the night as we moved from place to place in our spectacular, privileged but uncomfortable compartment. People of all economic levels wearing brightly coloured, and in most cases, beautiful clothing. Cows wandering around aimlessly as traffic was stopped to let them wander. Our train stopping to allow a cow on the tracks to stroll off, in its own time. We heard occasional music floating in the air. Palaces; Forts; lakes; bazaars; spices;

food; markets; wild tigers; and people everywhere. It was the experience that we had wanted. However, there was the reality also. The Indian reality. The second most populated country in the world.

There is a statistic which, once I had heard it, stuck in my head. In 1990, it was estimated that seventy per cent of people in India had no access to toilets. Since I first heard that in 2004, a new study in 2015 had stated that this was now down to sixty per cent. A vast and deliberate improvement. However, with over 1.3 billion people, India still has nearly 800 million people who go where they can find a place to go. And that can be anywhere. Why do I mention this? Only because I can say how that affects a beautiful train journey through Rajasthan, one of the loveliest places to travel in the world. As appalling as that statistic is, India has made huge progress in trying to solve the problem and therefore improving the health of everyone. We learned quite quickly not to throw back the cabin curtains first thing in the morning as we arrived in a new city. Otherwise, we would be greeted by literally hundreds of people sometimes, who lived along the tracks or around the stations. They had makeshift houses of wood and corrugated roofing and generally accepted open land toilet areas. They would wave enthusiastically at us no matter what they were doing. This, unfortunately, was also true in the streets of some cities we visited. It's a fact of life for them. It's a huge adjustment for us. After a few days, however, we ignored it and it didn't bother us (actually, it was just me who wasn't bothered).

Varanasi and a night in jail

Raam, Angie and Ali

After an emotional farewell to Raam and Ali with photos, hugs and handshakes, we flew to the holiest city in India. As we waited for our transport to Delhi airport, I saw across two platforms Raam and Ali greeting the new train guests. They were greeting them as fresh and enthusiastically as they had us. 'The King is dead, long live the King.' That is a talent I know I don't possess. To be able to switch off from one set of people as though they had never existed and to switch on to a new set as though they were the only ones in the world that had ever existed. They were two men who truly, and successfully, lived in the moment.

Varanasi, also known as Bañares, is situated on the bank of the River Ganges. Our general plan was to visit the house owned by Ravi Shankar, also the university and several notable temples. But our two prime reasons to travel to Varanasi were to go to Sarnath (the place where Buddha gave his first sermon) and, at dawn, to float along the Ganges in a boat to view the eighty or so Ghats. We were met by Ranjit and Mohammad, our assigned guides. The Ghats are stone steps leading down the west bank on the River Ganges. Towering above the Ghats are magnificent palaces and temples. Most Ghats are used for bathing and ceremonies, but two are for the sole purpose of cremation. All human life is there.

We stayed in a wonderful hotel; The Taj. Large walled grounds beautifully maintained. The restaurant had live Indian classical music each evening. The bedrooms were very comfortable, especially as we had just come from the rickety but splendid old train. We went to bed early as we had to get up before dawn. The boat trip along the Ganges was to start in the dark.

The boat turned out to be a small rowing boat, big enough for two people and a rower. We were to be rowed by our guide Ranjit's son, Adi. He was twelve years old. The three of us set off on the rowboat in pitch black with flaming torches lighting our way out into the enormous, black water of the river. Out from the river bank by about a hundred yards we lit candles placed in tiny boat-shaped vessels and floated them on the river. This is a Ganges ritual and is a moment to remember those family members who had passed away. Adi said a prayer. We could see many other lit candles floating along that others had launched that dawning morning. The current was moderate but awkward for Adi as it swirled rather than took any firm direction. I felt as though I should row the boat and that Adi should sit on Angie's knee.

The sun started to slowly light the sky from the other side of the river. It was a warm, pinkish colour that soon turned to

Adi rowing as dawn breaks on the River Ganges

blood red and then various shades of yellow in a blue sky. It was about five-thirty in the morning. The sun began to bring to life the wonderful site of the Ghats and temples along the riverbank. We made good progress as young Adi rowed us across the swirling water. The steps down to the water were already populated with bathers, people praying, eating, selling and talking. It was a fascinating sight and worth every bit of the effort in getting out of bed at four o'clock. After a while rowing, we came to two Cremation Ghats. Some 25,000 to 30,000 cremations take place on these Ghats every year. That's roughly eighty per day, every day of the year. Even more cremations are carried out in other parts of the city and the ashes brought to the Ganges for scattering onto the holy river. I haven't mentioned all those cremations that are performed in other parts of India and brought to Varanasi for scattering, as a pilgrimage for dead relatives. That's a lot of ashes scattered on the Ganges. Unfortunately, it is also somewhere where a lot of people bathe, dip their heads and generally immerse themselves. Just to add to the paradox and confusion in my mind, as our boat turned around to face the way back, I noticed the cremations were not wholly successful. I'm not saying any more about that. It was a truly unique Indian experience.

Rowing back was harder for Adi. There was a breeze now and the current seemed in direct opposition. We enjoyed the rest of the journey back, stopping once for fifteen minutes at the Dashashwamedh Ghat which is probably the most spectacular Ghat along the bank. There we met several Sadhu's — Indian monks who have renounced worldly life. The Sadhu's come every day to the river and wash, eat and pray. They also accept donations to allow them to lead their scant life. One gave me back some money as he thought it was too much.

After thanking Adi and offering a tip which he gladly took (and so he should), we were taken by Ranjit and our driver Mohammad to Ravi Shankar's house, where we saw the room he taught students while he was in his city of birth. This house was not where he was born. I'm a big fan of Ravi and have met him several times so I was particularly interested to see how he lived when in India. It was a short half an hour visit and we went on our way for one more stop at a temple. I forget the particular reason why this temple was picked, but there were two things that I remember from the visit.

Firstly, Macaque monkeys. They were everywhere and loved to dash about on the corrugated tin roofs of the houses next to the temple to snatch food and fruit from passers-by. They were loud, fearless and fairly vicious and possibly rabid. Being gravely sick in an Indian hospital wasn't on my bucket list. The second memorable moment of the temple visit was a huddle of around six or seven people outside the main door. They had leprosy. The kind where fingers and toes become disfigured and shortened. I put money in their baskets but did not make physical or eye contact. There is a quote I remembered from Helen Keller, "I cried because I had no shoes until I met a man who had no feet." Here, this was a reality.

We returned to our hotel for a really delicious meal, with a side dish of sitar and tabla. Before we went to bed a message found us at the bar. It was from Ranjit. It was short and to the point. He advised us to remain in the hotel the whole of the next day. Under no circumstances were we to leave the grounds. He finished his message by saying he would contact us in the morning to explain. At breakfast, he came to our table.

"Sorry, Mister Paul; sorry Misses Angela. We cannot go on our tour today," Ranjit was very upset, frantic and apologetic. I noticed Mohammad was not with him. Another driver, named Baz, had replaced him.

"Mister Paul, Lady Angela. We have a bad situation today. Yesterday a very, how you British say, high profile politician was murdered in his car. Most terrible. He was driving with his seven bodyguards and another car came alongside his car and opened fire, killing them all. Their bodies were taken down to the burning Ghats first thing this morning for cremation immediately. That is not quite normal to be that quick, but police thought it wise to have the cremations immediately to keep rioting under control. There are riots in the city. Bad riots with people going crazy for revenge. It's not safe for you to go to Sarnath today or anywhere. Please stay at your hotel."

"We leave tomorrow Ranjit so that means we miss seeing Sarnath and the university." I felt a bit miffed.

"Yes, so sorry Mister Paul and Lady Angela."

"Also, Ranjit where is Mohammad today?" I said plainly.

"Ah, Mohammad is in jail."

"What? In jail? What has he done?"

"Mohammad not done any bad things. He is very nice man, very good driver."

"Yes, we liked him very much. But why is he in jail?"

"He was arrested last night as the riots started and word got around about the assassination. Jail is a safer place."

"I don't understand, Ranjit. If Mohammad has done nothing wrong why did the police put him in jail?"

"Because Mister Paul, they wanted his car. You know the car we have been riding around in." Ranjit wasn't bridging our huge gap in comprehension of what the hell Mohammad had done to get thrown in jail.

"Don't worry, Mister Paul. Mohammad will only be in jail for one night, maybe two."

"Ranjit. Why did the police arrest Mohammad and put him in jail for one or two nights? Why did they want his car?" Straightforward questions. I waited for straightforward answers.

"Because his car is a big SUV. It is much higher up than any car the police have."

Angie and I waited for a full answer which was slowly being extracted. We just looked at him.

"OK, Mister Paul. Lady Angela. The police like

Mohammad's car very much. They also like Mohammad. Whenever there is trouble or going to be trouble, they confiscate his car and use its height to shoot at people through the windows. They say it's very handy. They do this about twice, maybe three times a year at most. They return it to Mohammad when the trouble is over. Any damage is corrected by the police."

"But why put him in jail?" I stubbornly persisted.

"Well, didn't you know? Mohammad is a Muslim. When riots happen here, and in a lot of places in India, Muslims are picked on. Sometimes they are killed. Very bad situations in some places. But the police here like our Mohammad. They take his car, put him in jail for his own protection. When things die down, he will have his car returned and can go back to his home. Very few Muslims are helped in this way. He is lucky." Helped and lucky would not have been my choice of words but I could see that it protected Mohammad.

We walked around the hotel grounds to kill some time. We did hear a lot of noise beyond the walls of the hotel. Angie spotted the hotel snake charmer sitting on the grass. I hate snakes so I decided to go back inside and read. Angie came back enthusing about the snake charmer. His cobra snake was double-headed. She had quite a show. He was part of the hotel entertainment between the hours of noon and sunset.

Snake charmer with two-headed Cobra

The next day, we had Baz and Ranjit turn up to take us to the airport for a flight back to Delhi. No Mohammad, and no Mohammad's car.

The three days we spent in Delhi were very touristy, including an intimidating trip through the streets of old Delhi in a hand-pulled buggy. We had never seen so many people in one small place. Old Delhi deserves another story just on its own.

As ever,
Paul

PS: We shared the wine box with the other two couples who shared our train carriage. They could not find wine they liked, including the wine the train stocked. Felix flirted with the idea of exporting decent wine to India. By the end of the trip, he had decided not to.

17. A perilous place to get married
Bali

Dear Brendan,

We accepted a wonderful wedding invitation from our friend Carl's daughter, Erin. It was to be Bali, in July. We hadn't been to Indonesia before and we were excited about discovering somewhere new. It was to be the first of five trips we have made to Bali; evidence that we fell in love with the island. What a wonderful place to get married. The wedding of Erin and Lucas was one of the best we've attended but for this story I thought you would like to hear about Balinese wedding preparations of an entirely different kind. Preparations which are ancient, unique and native to Bali. We were to enjoy an extraordinary and unexpected day.

An invitation to join a village

I thought I'd made a huge mistake when asking the man at the hotel reception desk about Bali. It turned out to be the best thing I could have done.

We had made friends with him the minute we checked into the Tanjung Sari hotel in Sanur. He invited us to have a chat with him after we'd settled in. He talked for quite a while and he covered all kinds of topics. We like to understand a bit about a place when we visit. I'll try to make it short and interesting.

Although Bali is part of Indonesia, the vast majority of

Balinese are Hindu's (pop. 4 million) whereas Indonesia is the largest Muslim country in the world (pop. 266 million). Our new friend at the hotel reception desk said, despite the strong differences between the religions, Balinese and the other Indonesians live very well together. Certainly, in Bali, tolerance of other people and their ways, prevails.

Balinese names are both simple and complicated. After listening to him as attentively as I could (plus some additional internet searches later) here is the explanation. Balinese people name their children depending on the order they are born, and the names are the same whether male or female. Simple.

However, the firstborn child is named Wayan, Putu or Gede, the second is named Made or Kadek, the third child goes by Nyoman or Komang, and the fourth is named Ketut. Slightly less simple. It helped us understand why the local coconut business along the beach was called 'Nyoman and Nyoman.' Wife and husband were both Nyoman. They had a son who worked with them and his first name was…Nyoman too.

If a family has more than four children, the cycle repeats itself, and the next 'Wayan' may be called Wayan Balik, which loosely translates to 'another Wayan'. Great, now I understand. Easy enough right?

But what about the people you meet who don't have one of these names? Some Balinese people have names that denote their caste or clan. For example, people from the Wesya (aristocratic) caste might be named Gusti, Dewa or Desak, people from the Ksatria (kings and warriors) caste are often called Ngurah, Anak Agung or Tjokorda, and people from the highest priestly caste, the Brahmana, are often named Ida Bagus for men or Ida Ayu for women. Jero indicates that a person, usually a woman, has married into a higher caste. OK, you are either bored ridged by now or you're hanging in there in the hope it's going to getter easier. Good luck with that but it will be worth it.

Just when you'd conquered it…you might run into people with names that don't fit into any of these categories. This is because they go by their nickname. With so many Wayans and Mades around, those tricky Balinese adopt nicknames to set themselves apart from the rest. Nicknames in Bali can be based on physical attributes such as Wayan Gemuk (fat Wayan), character traits like Ketut Santi (peaceful Ketut) or perhaps something arbitrary such as Wayan John or Made Legu (Made mosquito). At last, a fun bit for you to make up your own variations for some people you have loved, detested or just known to have a little quirk or two.

I looked at the name badge of our friendly concierge who had taken a long time and spent an inordinate amount of energy, on conveying this special system of naming. His name read 'Made Gemuk'; in other words, 'Fat Made'. I looked at him. He was tall and thin. I was about to run away when he said, "Ah Mister Paul, I see you are looking at my name. I was a fat baby. The name stuck." I liked the nickname convention. It was the easiest to remember.

We covered a lot of other topics including my questions on "why there were so many kites flying? How old were the traditional shadow puppets?" And the history of Gamelan music ensembles, etcetera. After a glass of mint tea, he asked us what we had planned during our stay. Made Gemuk then seemed to make a decision. I had the feeling that our discussion up to this point was in the form of an interview. It also seemed that we had passed.

"I would like to invite you to our village on Sunday," he said in a soft polite way. "The whole village is celebrating a Tooth Filing ceremony."

A whole day out

All we had to do, Fat (thin) Made said, was pay for someone to drive us to and from the village. We were invited to stay the whole day to include evening events. There was nothing for us to pay as we were guests and we could arrive and leave at any time. OK, but wait a minute, what the devil is tooth filing? Is it really filing a person's teeth? Well, yes, it is and the devil takes centre stage.

Balinese tooth-filing is an ancient custom that predates Hinduism's arrival on the island in the fifth century BC. These days, the old tradition has merged and evolved its culture, with tooth filing now reflecting a largely Hindu view of the human world. So what does that mean and why do they do it?

In Balinese culture evil traits such as greed, lust, confusion, anger, jealousy, stupidity, ill-will, and intoxication by either passion or drunkenness need to be controlled. They believe the fang-like nature of uneven teeth represent these evil traits. They believe filing them, to make them even, removes the desire for these traits.

Traditionally, it's important for tooth filing to be done when a boy or girl reaches puberty. If filing hasn't happened by the time they want to get married, it must be done before the wedding. After tooth filing, a father's duties to his female children are generally regarded as complete. If, for whatever reason, tooth filing hasn't taken place when someone dies then the teeth of the cadaver are filed before cremation. Balinese believe a person may be refused entrance to heaven if the teeth are not filed as they might be mistaken for ferocious witches, demons, wild animals, savages, or, almost as bad, dogs. The canine teeth are regarded as animalistic and fang-like.

Having your teeth filed is the most important event of adolescence. It is expected that the youngsters endure it without complaining. Tears may be shed but it expected that there should be no shouting or screaming. The Tooth Filing ceremony is expensive. Invitations must be issued, musicians are hired, the fee of the specialist Brahman priest (tooth filer) has to be paid, elaborate offerings are carried out, and a banquet is prepared for guests and villagers. For poorer people, the expense can be crippling.

Our ceremony was to include six people with teeth to be filed. They were going to share the cost equally and the whole village was invited. The money will have been saved by parents for years to do this. Sometimes financial help is offered to lower castes as current costs can reach around £2,000. Parents believe that youths of all castes cannot go on to lead healthy, well-adjusted lives as a part of Bali's tightly knit family, clan, community and society unless teeth filing has been carried out on their teenage children.

The Tooth Filing Ceremony

We were driven deep into the country, somewhere near the foot and shadow of Mount Agung, the highest point on the island. The mountain looked almost perfectly conical from where we were with clouds capping the peak. It dominates the region and even influences the weather, particularly rainfall, and is revered by the Balinese. In a way, it resembles Kilimanjaro in that it rises dramatically from flat, tropical terrain but on a somewhat smaller scale. From the top, you can look west and see the volcanoes of Java and east to the peak of Mount Rinjani on the island of Lombok. Mount Agung is an active volcano and every so often it erupts such that this village, and many others in this area, have to evacuate.

We took, on advice, small bamboo baskets with colourful offerings such as rice, sweet cakes, small flowers and fruits. The ceremony is always held on an auspicious day, however, it seemed to us that almost every day is some type of auspicious day in Bali. Although everyone else was dressed in traditional clothes, we were allowed to dress so that our heads, arms and bodies were covered. We both wore sarongs. Showing ankles and feet were permitted. It wasn't hard for us to stick to this requirement.

We arrived in the village and we were greeted by our new, thin friend Made Gemuk (Fat Made) and gifted a white cardboard box. Inside were snacks and sweetened tea. We were led to where the ceremony was to be held inside a large family compound. I will not explain the technicalities of Balinese family compounds, it's enough to say that traditionally the Balinese families live together in one compound, comprising several buildings, according to living requirements. This is to ensure that the young and old are all looked after by the whole family on a day to day basis. The village is close-knit and problems and opportunities are regularly shared between families. The meaning of the phrase "It takes a village to raise a child" is displayed, in reality, every day in Bali villages.

We noticed a makeshift bamboo shrine had been erected where the ceremony was to take place. Strong smelling incense pieces were burning in small fires, traditional music was played by a ten-strong traditional ensemble, comprising two metallophones played with mallets and sets of hand-played drums which keep time. I saw a xylophone and bamboo flutes ready to be played. We placed our offerings where others were placed, at the foot of the ceremony's temporary shrine.

We sat for a while just watching everyone. Small children were fascinated to see us, the only non-Balinese to be present. The whole village came in and out of the compound, singing, smiling, offering us small flowers for our hair or clothes. A strong, no, a very strong drink was being offered. I, of course, took one. Although people came up to us and spoke in their own language, it was obvious they were polite greetings and it was a warm welcome we were being given. Food and more drinks were offered and we took it. All we had brought with us was a camera. On advice from Fat Made we took no phones, no watches, nothing of modern technology except a decent camera.

I strolled around meeting villagers, we had no shared language but we did share smiles and nods and food and drink were offered by each person I said hello to. I was aware of the strength of the local drink and did not want to display an evil trait, such as drunkenness, as I might have ended up on the shrine having my uneven teeth sorted out. I discovered by accident a group of men squatting behind a wall. Gambling was underway. Dice were being thrown and a very unfamiliar sequence of moving wooden discs, solid-looking reeds and polished stones. Behind the men were caged cockerels. It suggested that maybe other forms of gambling were going to be taking place later that evening, but transported somewhere else. I saw pigs and chickens penned in, perhaps waiting for their inevitable end; probably to feed the villagers during the coming evening.

After an hour or two watching the villagers talking, we saw men and women parading in lines while passing the ceremony shrine singing old traditional songs or mantras. On their heads some women had elaborate crowns made from reeds and flowers, some had baskets of fruit and flowers. Everywhere were brightly coloured flowers. We saw many villagers, maybe a hundred. The whole time we listened and watched the ensemble joyously play their traditional music. The six initiates appeared dressed in white and gold clothing which signifies holiness. The two girls wore garments as beautiful as those worn by legong dancers (another part of Bali's ancient cultural traditions). The four males wore a single piece of cloth over their ceremonial clothes which reached from their armpits to their knees. At the back, the men had wavy-edged daggers protruding from a yellow sash.

The ceremony started after we had spent maybe two and a half hours absorbing the scene around us. It seemed to begin with holy water being sprinkled and the whole congregation blessing the group of six with well-practised mantras. The qualified, very expensive and healthy-looking 'dentist' wearing white stood next to the village 'mayor' wearing dark gold. Special offerings were being made to the gods of sexual love. Each initiate was to lay down in turn in the richly wrapped bamboo shrine cum platform. The first was a female. Not the youngest, she was at the back of the line of five waiting for their turn. The family gathered around the woman and she clutched a pillow and the 'dentist' lit some fresh incense. He provided some sort of mouthwash and set out his files and whetstones which he blessed, presumably asking them not to cause too much pain. He then put something in the corners of the girl's mouth and I later found out they were small cylinders of sugarcane to keep the jaws open and stop the person gagging. The actual filing lasted about fifteen minutes and the 'patient' was allowed a mirror to watch the progress being made. A yellow coconut half was provided to allow the 'patient' to spit out the filed pieces of upper canines. The 'dentist' talks to his files and whetstones as he works away. Presumably, this was to lift the spirits and atmosphere. People were laughing at what he was saying. Humour always helps a tense situation, doesn't it. When he'd finished, family members were asked to come on to the platform again to inspect his work. I was told later, by Fat Made, that some boys are asked to lie back again to have some extra strokes of the file to ensure the devil traits don't have any possibility to sneak back into their personality. When this poor girl was filed evenly, it was explained by our concierge, that she would be given the astringent betel pepper leaf to rub on the ends of the teeth after the 'dentist' had put a few soothing and healing tinctures on the end of her tongue. The coconut shell with her tooth bits and spit were going to be buried behind the family's shrine to avoid being occupied by the dreaded and much-feared evil spirits.

We saw the next filing ceremony of a young man and then left the village after finding Fat Made and thanking him. We felt unbelievably privileged. This day wasn't for tourists; it wasn't a show for foreigners; it wasn't superficial playacting. It wasn't for the faint-hearted participant or observer. It was something that was both intimate and private, but also open and inclusive. This experience connected all the senses. *Sight*; the rich colours of the offerings, the clothing, the flowers, the shrine the family courtyard, the act of filing teeth. *Hearing*; the live music from the ensemble, the wonderful singing, the chanting of mantras, the continuous ringing of the small prayer bell, the laughter of the children excited at the big village event. *Smell*; incense burning in small fires, food preparation and aromatic cooking. *Taste*; the food and drink. *Touch*; the feel of the beautiful woven silk adorning the filing shrine, the warm, dry hands of the people greeting us. All of this at the same time feeling part of, and welcomed into, a way of life we could never have known about, or had any chance of experiencing other than at the generous invitation of Fat Made.

If Fat Made visited England, I would struggle to think of anything that would be the equivalent. Anything that would show him our ancient way of living. A cathedral, Stonehenge, museums showing some of our history, of course, but nothing that is integral to the current way we live. Nothing that would stimulate all the senses. No tradition that has lasted for five hundred years before Christ.

We didn't see Fat Made for the next two days and then we had to move on. We didn't see him again. These days, we smile to ourselves when we see Bali advertised as a wedding destination.

As ever,
Paul

PS: We were encouraged to take photos of the whole day's events, including a film of the actual tooth filing. Every so often we watch it.

Waiting for their turn

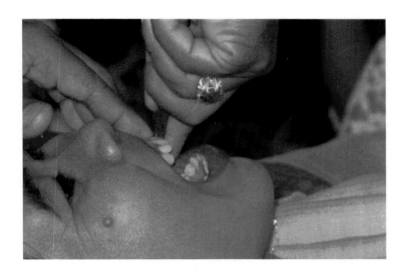

Rubbing the betel pepper leaf on the filed teeth to sooth them
Watching the event, having a good time

The Blue Mosque, Istanbul

18. Pioneering Istanbul

Dear Brendan,

It was February 2000. I arrived at my London office from the 6:37 am train. It was still dark and raining hard. I was cold, wet and miserable. The day was to get worse.

I've never fallen in love with a city, at least not on the first visit. A city usually grows on you in a series of particular moments. To me, to love a city requires a deep appreciation and/or respect for its style, architecture, art, music, food, drink, smells, how the inhabitants go about their lives and how they treat each other and how they treat strangers. Ultimately, for me, the love for a city means I could live there without question. Istanbul comes close to it but I don't think I could live there, full time.

I'm not actually writing to you about Istanbul. This story is about what happened during a twenty-four-hour period while in the city.

The short phone call

We had been working in Istanbul, in multiple teams, for about three years. Seven different banks had employed our teams to help bring their operations in line with the best practices of western banks. Our work had been going extremely well and everyone was happy. Our customers; the local corporation team; my bosses; the teams from London; everyone was happy! Until that morning.

My phone rang and I picked up what I thought was to be another mundane call. It was Hasan, the senior contact executive for the Bank where we had made our first breakthrough contract in Istanbul.

"Paul, I want to see you in my office please; first thing tomorrow morning. I shall expect you at around eight o'clock." He hung up before I could ask the obvious. I rang my senior project manager, Fred, in the bank. He said he didn't know why Hasan would ask for a meeting. I asked him to find out while I was making immediate travel plans and rearranging everything that was scheduled that day and the next. I could get a Turkish Airline flight that afternoon, arriving just before midnight. I could see Hasan the next day as requested, sort things out, and get back to London on the last flight with another airline. Two flights, one hotel and taxis. It was sorted out quickly but I'd given plenty of time for Fred to sniff out the reasons for the phone call but nothing was forthcoming. Hasan was not to be disturbed all day. I was going completely blind into what was obviously going to be a very difficult situation. Hasan had never had less than a fifteen-minute chat with me. Not ever.

I had known him for two years and we had become good friends. We trusted each other implicitly. Good, sustainable trust. One that is proven through each other giving up something important because it was in the other person's interest. I had learned that trust can evaporate in seconds with the wrong action, suggestion or even just neglect. So the correct response to his request was paramount.

I arrived at Istanbul airport at one o'clock in the morning local time. It was cold, windy and raining hard. I got in a yellow taxi, front seat as the back doors weren't opening. My driver, who looked at least eighty years old, drove like a maniac. We sped along the wet, greasy motorway into the city at about eighty miles an hour. But that wasn't what started me worrying. As we accelerated, with the drivers foot flat to the floor, I noticed he was beginning to fall asleep. I nudged him with my elbow and he jerked awake and accelerated again. His head began to droop. I nudged him, he jerked awake. This happened another five times. I did not take my gaze from him until we arrived at the hotel. What dire circumstances must exist to make an eighty-year-old man drive a taxi at eighty miles an hour, on wet, greasy roads at 1 o'clock in the morning? Survival? I couldn't see how it would help him survive very long. Maybe he had been driving like that for his whole life. I thanked him, paid him and went to bed thanking God that the back doors of the taxi didn't open.

The first meeting

I walked into Hasan's office at eight o'clock precisely. Çay (tea) was offered and we swapped pleasantries but it was obvious we were going through the civilised part of the meeting. He was warm and smiling as usual. Then, after the normal amount of time (probably five minutes) for a Turkish non-contentious opening, his face changed and I went into heavy listening mode.

"Paul, one of your team from London was married this weekend." Serious face.

"Oh, really?" I had no idea what he was talking about. "He was married in the grounds of the hotel."

"I didn't know, I'm surprised no one told me," I said stalling for time, wishing he would get on with telling me what the problem was.

"It was Jonty Mitchell." I was wondering why he was doing this to me. It must have been obvious I had no idea what this was about.

"Ah, Jonty. Yes, he's known to keep his private life quiet." This was driving me mad. No matter how much I wanted to ask him to get to the point I knew enough to let Hasan continue in his own way and at his own speed.

"Paul, Jonty Mitchell got married this weekend, to another man, at this bank's expense. I want to know what you are going to do about it. Today!"

The nub of the problem

I cannot explain in this letter what a thunderbolt that was and just how unprepared I was for this situation. Part of our contract agreement with the Bank included them paying for my London team's expenses. Hotels, meals and flights would be the Bank's expense. It was agreed individually that they could return home to London every two weeks or their spouses/partners could fly to Istanbul for the equivalent cost instead. Not a problem it would seem, until now. Ninety-eight per cent of Turkish people are Muslims. The Bank was owned and operated by a Muslim family. Jonty was gay but there was nothing illegal about that in Turkey. However, same-sex couples have no legal recognition there. OK, so that was the legal situation. Let's just say homosexuality does not currently sit well with the Islamic religion and at that time, in the year 2000, even in Britain it was not talked about or recognised so openly and positively in employment situations as it is today. Jonty had asked his partner to spend the weekend with him, in his hotel bedroom, sharing his meals, on the Bank's expense account including his flight. Not illegal, but as Jonty had not consulted anyone as far as I could tell, or even discussed with anyone whether this was appropriate behaviour, it was clearly a huge cultural embarrassment to all concerned. That's not to mention that he and his partner had a same-sex marriage in the hotel grounds with someone recognised by their London community as a credible official. In 2000, in the UK, nothing had been passed into law recognising civil partnerships (came into effect in 2005) or same-sex marriage (came into effect 2013). Jonty and his partner were pioneering. Pioneering is definitely one way to get the change that is needed but in a Muslim country? At the expense of a Muslim family-owned bank? Pioneers have a history of getting arrows in their backs.

To make matters worse for my sweating brain, our corporation had publicly stated its intent to extend domestic partner benefits to gay and lesbian employees in the U.S. that year and the expectations were that it be part of its "Equal

Opportunity Policy" worldwide soon. This moment was in the 'in-between' world. I was between the proverbial rock and a very, very hard place. My personal opinion wasn't going to count.

The long phone call

I called the Human Resource Director back in London. She wasn't available. I was put through to a senior manager, Henry, in the HR department. I explained the situation. Henry was very quiet, didn't interrupt and was silent.

"So, Henry, what is your advice?" I asked calmly.

"Best do nothing until someone gets back to you. Where will you be in the next few days?"

"Henry, tonight I'm going to either be in London at ease and sleeping contentedly like a baby or I'm going to be in London explaining to my boss and probably a few others why we had just been thrown out by a prestigious customer, with whom we have built a fantastic relationship, and had a twenty-million dollar contract cancelled."

"I think you are telling me that you have to make a decision pretty quickly." Henry was showing me that he catches on, eventually. "Well, Paul, make sure you do the right thing by everyone." I stared at the phone in my hand and mouthed several, silent, swear words, several times, as Henry waited for my answer.

"Henry, could I ask you to please put me through to Morris, my boss. Thank you." I was still calm. I waited.

"Hello, Morris Carter." Mo had a flat, unemotional voice. He was forty-five-years-old, completely bald and had the empathy of the Berlin Wall. I'd overheard one of my team call him a "baby-eater" recently. It was an interesting if a little strong, description. I took another ten minutes to explain the situation to Morris. He reacted differently from Henry. Morris snorted, puffed out air and sucked his teeth. Occasionally, he whispered loudly "fuck" as I brought him up-to-date.

"I've talked to Henry, in HR. Julie, the Director of HR wasn't available to take my call. Henry told me to do nothing and wait to be called back. I don't believe this is an option for me today." I stated factually.

"Too fucking right! Whatever happens, I don't want any problems with the customer or the contract, all right? AND I don't want this getting out into the rest of the bank and marketplace. Do you hear me? It will kill our numbers in our Eastern European performance stats. What's more, if this gets out, customers and, even worse, competitors in the Middle-East are going to kill us! You and I might actually get fired. Or worse, we'll end up with managing some fucking remote corner of the back of beyond!" Morris was reacting differently from Henry, I could tell!

"OK, thank you, Morris. I'll let you know." I rang off. Well, let the record show I tried the right places for advice. I wrote down what was said in those two phone calls and who said it. From experience, this was a good thing to do.

I walked slowly to where our project team was located on the customer's site. The sky was a grey and it was raining. I got wet going from one building to the next. I had, at this point, no idea what to do. I met my Project Manager, Fred. He was in charge of operating almost every aspect of the work with the customer and he was very good at it. Also, most importantly, I liked him and trusted him.

"Good morning, Fred." Fred looked up from his screen and looked a little surprised to see me at first and then he remembered my phone call the day before. He got up to shake my hand and asked if I wanted a Turkish coffee or Çay or something else.

"A bit early for something else," I said. He squeezed out a strangled laugh from the back of his throat. He was clearly a little nervous as to why I was there. I could tell he was thinking that I usually only turned up to do an 'executive front end and back end' to a final report on projects, and/or to sell another project. So, something was up.

"Can we find somewhere for a quiet chat?" I asked.

We found an office and I told him the whole story, including the long phone call to London to Henry and the lovely Morris just a few minutes ago. I was conscious of trying not to be transparent and pointing fingers so I explained that both Henry and Morris each had their own positions to defend.

"Bullshit!" came the steady but loud response from Fred. That's my boy, I thought but did not react, mainly because I didn't want my own thoughts on the subject to suddenly burst through from my toes in waves of expletives. If I did that it would give an excuse for anyone else to do it too. It's OK, I can survive this. No problem. But how? I was more than a mile away from rational thinking at this point.

"Paul, I didn't know. Truthfully, I didn't know. I'm sorry perhaps I should have done but…" I stopped him.

"Fred. You didn't know Jonty was gay. I didn't know Jonty was gay. What is more important is that no one, not you, not me, could have guessed this could possibly have happened. Sometimes difficult things just happen and we've got to sort them out the best way we can. No good going around blaming people or though I'm beginning to think I'm going to fire Jonty. This is unforgivable behaviour." For a moment, I let my

257

guard drop and Fred could see I was angry. "The whole thing was unnecessary and could have been handled in a better way, for Jonty too.

"Paul, don't fire him! He is good at what he does. He has been thoughtless. Give him a break. Please." I took what he said and didn't react.

"OK, Fred. Let me think about it. If he wasn't on the project who would be a good replacement?" I got the answer I was looking for and asked Fred to go back to the Project building and I'd call him and let him know my decision. I also requested that he send Jonty Mitchell to come and see me in the office I was in. I asked Fred not to mention our discussion to anyone. I knew I could trust him.

Jonty

During the half an hour I waited to see Jonty I had to think clearly about what action to take. I struggled. Why was I in the middle between western social change, religious sensitivities, changing corporate attitudes, human rights recognition, my customer sensitivities and my own business objectives and professionalism? Then I thought I was being very pompous and I should just get on and make a decision that's based on instinct and live with it. Then it came to me as Jonty walked in.

"Hello, Jonty. Do you know why I'm here?"

"I suppose, to sell some more work or something."

"OK, well I'll come straight to the point. I understand you organised a wedding last Saturday, for you and your male partner, in the hotel, in a Muslim country, essentially funded by the Muslim family-owned Bank we are working in currently."

He looked shocked and slightly irritated. "What's wrong with that? I didn't use the expense budget for anything I wasn't allowed to do. It says I can have my spouse or partner over to Istanbul instead of going home. The corporation is recognising rights for people like me. Are you saying I have no right to have my wedding ceremony wherever I want?"

I refused to go down the path of giving Jonty a debate on rights and wrongs and how that was changing. It wasn't going to help.

"Jonty, in this particular situation I have to do what is best. The dominant factor for my decision is that I must put the customer first. That is the first of our corporations stated values. You have put the customer in an extremely difficult position. What's more, unless I act in a very quick and positive manner for the customer, Hasan will be, most probably, fired from his job at the bank. It will smear him personally and, in this city, information is passed extremely quickly, especially negative information. The bank will most likely get smeared and its business will most probably suffer. You didn't ask if this was acceptable. Not from Hasan, not from anyone in the bank, not from Fred your immediate Project Manager and not from me. You put yourself first without regard to the customer. Jonty, you know how these things are regarded in this country at this time, you're not stupid. So, in this situation, I think you have abused the privileges offered by our customer and damaged your reputation and that of our corporation. I have to repair that damage by putting the customer first. I have to avoid any damage to our customer. I want you to clear all your belongings, arrange for a flight back to London today, go to your hotel and check out. I will be in touch next week about your next assignment."

He showed his anger. "What? Are giving me the sack?"

"No, Jonty I'm moving you to another assignment next week. As you know, that is the very nature of the job we do. Please take a couple of days off, if you want to. Until I call." I delivered my last words to him slowly, calmly and, very firmly. However, I wasn't as calm or as assured as I tried to appear.

"I'm going to sue the company; I'm going to sue you. I've got my rights and I'll drag you through the employment tribunals!" He shouted.

I got up, opened the office door and stood waiting for him to leave. If it's possible to sweat inwardly, I was doing it at that point. I'm human too, I thought.

He left and I went to Hasan's office immediately. I was asked to go straight in to see him.

Hasan

He stood up from behind his desk, came round to my side and shook my hand. His face was expressionless.

"Hasan, I have understood as much as I needed in order to make a decision. Jonty will have left the bank's premises within an hour. He will be replaced by Greg Barker, a specialist in the same area as Jonty. Greg will start on Monday, with your approval. The project team will be told that Jonty was needed on another project, in the UK, next week. All the fees for Jonty's work to date will be refunded to the bank as will any and all expenses incurred by Jonty and anyone associated with Jonty's private life that have been charged or accrued to the bank. The bank will not pay a single dollar for any of Jonty's involvement. However, Jonty's work was his usual high standard for the bank and that stays as part of the value we bring to this project. Have we gone some way to remedying this situation?"

Hasan, who was quite a bit shorter than me, came towards me, grabbed my hand and tried to kiss me on both cheeks. The whole physical movement was a bit awkward and we both were a bit uncomfortable so I leant downwards enough for him to succeed. Of course, men kissing both cheeks, was completely normal in Turkey but this was the first time he'd tried it on me, an Englishman. We both stepped back quickly after the brief encounter.

"Thank you. I will go to see Hakan, our CEO, now. This episode will get out so he needs to know how we have dealt with it. Please come and see me before you go to your flight back today," he said.

Returning

I had lunch with Fred, the Project Manager and told him what was happening and what was needed. He was relieved. He would adjust the fees and expenses and he was very clear on what I had asked him to do. He was also happy with Greg Barker as a replacement.

After lunch, I called my warm and cuddly boss, Morris. I told him what I had done and why and how the customer had reacted so far.

"Ok. Good. I assume you have already cleared this with HR?"

"Er, not yet, Morris. I thought I'd do it in order of importance, so I called you first." I was trying to bring a little light relief to the conversation but as we all know, 'some fall on stony ground'. I imagined Morris with a stony face at that moment.

"Well, I can't approve what you've done until HR think you haven't broken any laws or corporate business practices. Only call me again once you've ok'd it with them," he blurted.

"OK, Morris. I'll call HR. I'll let you know when the coast is clear." He may have missed my subtlety. Thankfully.

So at this point, I'm thinking of a quote from the Alfred, Lord Tennyson poem, 'Charge of the Light Brigade':

"Cannon to right of them, cannon to left of them, cannon in front of them."

I was the cannon target. The Battle of Balaclava took place just the other side of the Black Sea from where I was.

When I made my next call, I was passed to Henry again by the HR Director's secretary for 'continuity reasons'. I told him about my decision and action.

"But I told you to wait until you get a call!" he squealed. "You can't just make a decision like that on your own."

"Henry, my dear old thing. Not only can I, but most importantly, I have. Circumstances determined I should do something positive for the customer and try and secure our business contracts and relationships today. I did make this clear. You may not be aware but we are two hours ahead of you here and no sign of the cavalry coming to my rescue from HR." I was warming to my theme of the men on horses going into battle. It helped my morale significantly. "Henry, what's more, I have transferred Jonty to another project starting next week and I've given him a few days off if he wants them. Why not call Morris and chat it through with him?"

"Shit, I'm not speaking to that grumpy sod."

"OK, Henry I'm going to catch my plane home now." I hung up.

I confirmed Jonty and Greg Barker's re-assignments. I

was about to ask for a taxi when Hasan appeared, told me he'd got his driver to take me to the airport. He joined me in the back of his very nice Audi. I made a joke about saving the bacon. Mine, his, Jonty's and Morris's. I can't remember the bacon joke anymore but I'm sure it was in poor taste in front of a Turk.

Returned

I arrived back in Terminal 4, Heathrow, "tired and emotional" as the saying goes. The flight had been late taking off, and it was past midnight. Jonty was not on my flight but I'd noticed the politician David Owen, that is Lord Owen to most people, had been on the flight. He'd kept himself to himself on board. Neither of us had had to wait for checked luggage so we had gone straight through to the arrivals' hall. It was empty. I was expecting Malcolm, my tried and trusted taxi driver, to be there but he wasn't. Lord Owen looked similarly disappointed. It was the last flight into Terminal 4 that night. The passengers with luggage all filed through and out into the car park or waiting family or friends. It was just Lord Owen and me. I called Malcolm's number for the third time to get the same "Please leave a message," an unhelpful phone mantra. Lord Owen just stood still.

A slightly dishevelled, heavily sweating and limping Malcolm came stumbling through the airport door and straight over to me. I remember a noiseless Lord Owen moving in Malcolm's direction, halt, move back and then slump a little while still standing as upright as he could.

"Sorry I'm a bit late, Paul," Malcolm began. "Been up since five this morning doing various airport runs and fell asleep in the car park waiting for your plane to get in." Poor man. He was in his early sixties, overweight and unhealthily flushed. The thin strands of his dirty grey hair matted to his head. He tried to take my small carry-on bag but I won the tussle on that one. Another driver appeared in uniform, including a smart cap. He came hurrying into the (almost) empty hall. He staggered up to the woman at the information desk. After a quick discussion, she made an announcement over the terminal speaker. It echoed loudly in the (almost) empty building.

"Would Lloyd Owen please come to the information desk." A pause. "Lloyd Owen?" The request echoed again.

Lord Owen did not move. His jaw muscles clenched tightly. Both Malcolm and I spotted what was afoot. There were five people in the vast arrivals building; Malcolm, the new smart driver, the information desk person, Lord Owen and me. Malcolm and I waited to see what would happen. Dead silence for about half a minute. Pride was winning, the Lord was losing.

"Would Lloyd Owen please come to the information desk. Lloyd Owen."

I was much too tired for more fun, so I walked over to the information desk where the driver stood.

"I think you'll find that Lloyd is standing over there," I offered helpfully.

Malcolm and I waited until we were out of the building and into the chilly, fresh night air before bursting out laughing.

As ever,
Paul

Notes:

If anyone from Harvard Business Review is reading this then you should know that my fees are very reasonable for using this story (or a more eloquent version of it). Lecturing, of course, will require a special deal to be negotiated.

Jonty did not sue anyone. I'm very pleased that there were no "No win, no fee" employment tribunals then.

We were to get many more projects with Hasan. We increased the number of different customers in Istanbul to eight in the next two years.

I may not have recorded, in this letter, the chat between Jonty and me with the precise wording used by either of us.

No one in Human Resources called me about this situation and Morris didn't mention it except in my annual review. That mention was positive, for Morris anyway. He got a different job in the corporation six months later. And so did I.

19. They are blowing up the beach Scotland

Dear Brendan,

It started with a kiss. I left Angie waving goodbye. It was early. Probably, five in the morning. I was going to the birthplace of dynamite.

I drove to Heathrow and caught a flight to Glasgow. I hired a car and started towards the Ayrshire coast, heading for Paisley. As I drove out of Glasgow, I started to see houses and businesses thin out along the road and the colour green dominated everywhere I looked.

It was October 1988. I had been seconded to ICI for a year to help develop their global electronic messaging, email and document management into a compatible service for all the different parts of the conglomerate. Basically, dull as ditchwater stuff today but, believe it or not, almost pioneering for big companies in those days to have employees pervasively connected by computer networking. It even sounds odd calling it computer networking now.

My mission that day was to meet important people and influential people, (not always the same people I had learned) in Nobel's Explosives, a company originating from the famous

Alfred Nobel.[8] This business was part of the network of companies owned by Imperial Chemicals Industries (ICI), a huge conglomerate of multiple and highly individual companies that covered the whole globe. The history of companies is pretty boring to everyone except the company boards and public relations departments. I needed to know something about each place I went to in order to do my job. I had to help them decide priorities and write a plan to implement them. Not one company of the ICI conglomerate had this in their top ten priorities. Only the corporate HQ considered it important. As I soon found out.

Establishing a plan was the objective for my year-long loan to them. Being a straightforward person, I'd assumed, at first, this was what was wanted and agreed by all. In reality, I spent most of my time selling the idea; convincing the doubters; proving cost-effectiveness to the accountants; showing how it would help workflow (later to be called processes) and take away the fear of change and new technology. ICI was full of chemists, research pharmacists and highly technical people who were yet to be convinced that computers could help them beyond the traditional accounting, personnel departments or certain specialist areas of research. In many ways, this company was still a fragment of the British Empire. On one site I visited, there was a hierarchy of nine separate canteens, cafeterias or restaurants. It depended on your job status as to where employees and management could

---

[8] Alfred Nobel discovered dynamite by accident. He first produced it in the factory at Ardeer in the town of Stevenston, Scotland. When his brother died newspapers published Alfred's obituary by mistake. He was so upset at being negatively viewed through his discovery and production of dynamite that he set up a trust to establish the Nobel Prize. He set aside the majority of his wealth for this. He wanted to leave a better legacy. His relatives only found out he had done this following his death.

eat lunch. The information technology departments were mistrusted and resented just about everywhere I went. Not surprisingly, I was mistrusted and resented just about everywhere I went. That is quite a challenging environment. I was, however, getting paid to do my utmost best. Getting paid was my highest priority.

Arriving at Nobel's Explosives, I was allowed onsite via a guarded entrance gate. There was a high perimeter fence as far as I could see. I don't remember any detail about the actual layout of the site. I parked and someone collected me from reception to take me to the first meeting. Whenever I visited a new part of ICI, and before I left base camp in Manchester, I always had a briefing containing three things. Firstly, the company's history. Secondly, a confidential hint as to its importance in the grand scheme of things (i.e. the likelihood of it remaining in the ICI Group or being sold off), therefore how important it was to what I was trying to do. Lastly, who to talk to and who to be nice to and who to ignore no matter what their job title or assumed status. Things can change very quickly I was told. I detected company ownership, job positions and priorities could change pretty quickly but installing common email and electronic document systems would be slow!

The first two meetings that day went according to plan and expectation. The third was to be the last and it was not even lunchtime. Very loud explosions could be heard coming from the beach area. I showed considerable alarm.

"Hey, dornt ya werry little laddie. 'tis the boys testing some new types of explosives. Happens all the time. They do it on the beach. There's nay werry." I was being calmed by the head of this particular meeting.

However, as I tried to focus on the ins and outs of rolling out the computing connection plan for Nobel's Explosives, bells started ringing. Not in my head but outside. Then a very loud siren started its slow deep drone and went quickly into a high-pitched shriek. People got up from their desks and started to close all the poorly maintained windows.

"What's happening now?" I called out trying to be heard.

"It's a toxic gas alert. Quite dangerous. If you want to leave the site today, then it has to be in the next few minutes as they will close the gates to anyone going in or out. This happens maybe twice a year. Unluckily for you, it's happening today. We might have to stay here until late this evening or until it's safe to go out. If you're going, then get going!"

I had nowhere booked to stay for the night. I ran to my car having furiously packed my papers and overhead projection transparencies. I jumped in amid deafening noise and turmoil as everyone, except me, was running into special areas made for just the purpose of protecting against a toxic gas escape. I could still hear explosions coming from the beach.

I reached the guard at the gate who was just shutting and locking the gate. He let me through and shouted, "Better drive fast laddie, the wind is blowing in your direction!" He was smiling so I assumed he knew I was English.

As I sped through Ardeer and the town of Stevenston, there was another siren sounding. I assumed it was to warn the town inhabitants of the toxic storm headed their way. Windows were shut, doors were slammed. My hands-free mobile phone rang. It was Angie. "Hello, are you having a nice business lunch? Er, what's that sound?"

"Sirens. Must be a fire practice," stay calm, I thought, and she won't know a thing. Then a very loud explosion happened, coming from the beach area.

"What the hell was that!" she shouted. Before I could think properly, I blurted out, "They're blowing up the beach. They do it every day. I'm in luck, I think I can catch an earlier

flight as I'm leaving Nobel's now. I'll keep you posted. Bye."
Click.

I drove hard and saw no one on the road until I reached the main road taking me back to Glasgow Airport. I had no such luck with getting an earlier flight. I sat and watched three men stand at the bar in Glasgow airport and drink four pints of 'heavy' each before they boarded the same flight as me.

I arrived home at around midnight. The day finished with a kiss.

As ever,
Paul

PS: In 2002, Nobel Enterprises was bought by a Japanese firm.

PPS: Between 1988 and 2008 ICI bought and sold several companies. In 2008 ICI was bought by a Dutch company who immediately sold off parts and integrated the rest with its own multi-part businesses.

PPPS: Every now and then I wonder whether my efforts were worthwhile during that year. I fool myself most of the time into thinking they did, a bit.

PPPPS: In my experience, in order to make change happen, you must have three strong factors in your favour.

1. A compelling reason for the change.
2. A collective will to make it happen.
3. Leaders personally committed to driving the change.

Number three is like bacon and eggs. The chicken was involved but the pig was committed. There were a lot of chickens that year.

20. Arrested
Everglades City, Florida

Dear Brendan,

We drove into Everglades City for the first time in 1988. I wanted to leave immediately and Angie wanted to live there.

I'm going to reveal the story of this city and some of its past inhabitants and you can make up your mind which camp you might fall into. I think I'd know.

Wildlife and terrain

Florida's Everglades National Park is a rare and natural wilderness. The area around Everglades City is a 2,000 square mile saltwater labyrinth comprising mangrove keys known as the Ten Thousand Islands. If you travel for an hour and twenty minutes along the Tamiami Trail (Route 41), going west from Miami, you'll pass Joanie's Blue Crab Café sitting at the roadside, in the middle of nowhere. Another ten minutes will bring you to Route 29 where you turn left and go due south. In a further ten minutes driving, you'll then find yourself in Everglades City. It is eighty-five miles west of Miami and thirty-six miles southeast of Naples, Florida in the middle of a sub-tropical, natural wilderness. It borders the Gulf of Mexico and the Ten Thousand Island National Wildlife Refuge. A further eight miles along the only road in and out of town you can find the small island of Chokoloskee and then you have reached a dead-end. If you thought Everglades City was the "Last Frontier Town" you should see Chokoloskee. Chokoloskee Island is a shell mound, built roughly 20 feet (6 m) high over thousands of years of occupation by the Calusa (meaning 'fierce people') Indian Tribe. The contents of the mound will most likely be animal bone, human excrement, botanical material, mollusc shells, potsherd, and lithic.

In this remote area, you have to keep a serious lookout for Alligators, Crocodiles, Panthers, Burmese Pythons, Eastern Diamondback Rattlesnakes, Eastern Indigo snakes and one or two Cottonmouth snakes. Raccoons, of course, are everywhere and despite looking cuddly and cute are vicious and can be rabid. Black Bears are a rare sight but do like to rummage through waste bins for food, particularly at Joanie's Blue Crab Café just down the road. The area is isolated and the greatest roadless wilderness in America. This place is not for the faint-hearted.

Weather conditions

Everglades City and Chokoloskee have around eighty to one hundred inches of rain a year (southern England is about 25 inches a year) and the average temperature in the summer months is 32-35 degrees Celsius (90–95 degrees Fahrenheit). From April to November, the humidity is unbearable and the mosquitos (sometimes called 'Swamp Angels') infest every nook and cranny (and that's just on your body). Today, the town is still recovering from Hurricane Irma's floods, which made landfall on Sunday, September 10, 2017. It was estimated that three-quarters of homes were flooded, many of which had no flood insurance. This was the most recent of a long list of hurricanes and tropical storms to hit the area. As

I've said, this place is not for the faint-hearted.

A bank arrives and then leaves

In 1923, Barron Gift Collier, the founder of Collier County, turned a small, sleepy fishing and farming village and trading post into a vibrant, modern town. Within five years, he established roads, including finishing the famous Tamiami Trail, the first east-west road across the Everglades. He had established a railroad, a bank, a telephone, sawmills, a boatyard, churches, a school, workers' barracks and mess halls, and even its own streetcar at one time. His idea was to set up a lucrative sportsman's paradise. He founded the famed Rod and Gun Club which still operates today and has had visits from such well-known people as Ernest Hemingway and Mick Jagger, although I'm pretty sure they didn't come together. More of that later.

The most noticeable and attractive building in town is the old Bank of Everglades. The bank building is situated just along from the City Hall in the middle of town. I mention this bank because of what is known about its customers in those days. The bank was housed in a beautiful building, in a beautiful wilderness but in a notorious city.

It was to be the bank for the 'one-man-city business'. The bank received its charter in 1923 and moved into this spectacular building in 1927.

From Everglades City's early surge in development, things took a big dip through the Great Depression where the main source of income for the town resorted to more 'pre-Collier' traditional ways; rum-running from the Bahamas; wildlife poaching; and farming. However, in 1962 when Colliers business in the area had long since dwindled away, the bank moved to Immokalee forty-two miles away and eventually became part of the Florida Community Bank. During the period 1927 to 1962 the bank supported the local community. A local community that began to increase through a mix of bank robbers and general outlaws. Men on the run were very well protected by the Everglades wilderness. A haven for types wanting to disappear from their previous lives. Infamous outlaws like "Bloody" Ed J. Watson, who had killed over fifty of his plantation workers to avoid paying their wages. He would vanish into wilderness hideaways to avoid capture and reappear later when the heat was off. There are many stories of lawmen coming to the area, hunting wanted criminals and then disappearing, not to be seen again. I could speculate but I don't know exactly what happened to them. Nobody does.

The building left behind by the bank was used as a boarding house until 1979 when the local weekly newspaper, Everglades Echo, moved in. In 1988, it was sold and has been used as a Bed & Breakfast since then. So, although the history of the bank ends there, what I find interesting is where it was set, its probable customers and the type of outlaw community it served through prohibition, bootlegging and the depression.

The locals and the local economy

The area around Chokoloskee Bay, including the site of Everglades City, was occupied for thousands of years by Native Americans of the Glades culture, who were absorbed by the Calusa tribe shortly before the arrival of Europeans as the New World developed. But by the time Florida was transferred from Spain to the United States in 1821, the area was uninhabited. The Calusa had been wiped out by a combination of war with rival tribes coming from Georgia and South Carolina and diseases brought by the Europeans. Today, the Seminole and Miccosukee tribes occupy southern and south-west Florida and have large areas of land allocated by the federal government for their Reservations. The Seminole tribe has been particularly successful with its Hard Rock and Casino Resort (the tribe bought the Hard Rock franchise with cash). Both tribes prosper from gambling in this part of Florida. Everglades City and Chokoloskee are not part of any tribal territory or Reservation land.

As I've mentioned, Europeans established themselves through fishing, hunting and trapping at the beginning of the 20th century. 'Boom' (Collier development) and 'Bust' (Great Depression) had shaped the local economy but had no serious effect on the main body of the residents as they always had the abundant wildlife to fall back on for food and commerce. At the 2016 census, the population was 411 (up by 7 on the previous 2013 census). 97% of the residents were white. The first census in 1930 showed 172 inhabitants which peaked in 1950 to 625 and started to fall away to its current level due to two factors. Colliers business declined in the area and the establishment of the Everglades Nation Park in 1947. At the time the Park was founded, and therefore under government control, the main source of income for the inhabitants of the Ten Thousand Islands had been hunting and commercial fishing. With the new status came a new reality for the residents. Hunting Alligators and all other types of natural wildlife was to come to an end. This was a devastating blow. The only fishing areas allowed were outside of the Park boundaries in the open sea of the Gulf of Mexico and Florida Bay. Families who had been established for generations knew nothing else but how to survive on the land and waters in this unique area. What were they to do?

Many kept (illegally) hunting and fishing until Alligators were declared an endangered species. The plain and straight forward people started to take more risks with the law and one or two started smuggling marijuana. What happened next can best be explained through the life of the Ten Thousand Islands most famous resident, Loren G. "Totch" Brown.

Totch's Place
(Courtesy Clyde Butcher, Venice Gallery, Florida)

Totch

Totch Brown was a local folk hero. Born on Chokoloskee Island in 1920, he was a fourth-generation resident of the area.

His father was the local taxidermist for hunters who wanted to sell their mounted wildlife to the rich and to top hotels in the north. He also ran a moonshine business during the Prohibition period. Both sets of grandparents had helped establish and develop the community. His great-grandfather John J. Brown had settled here in 1880 and his maternal grandfather, Charles G. McKinney, came to this last frontier of Florida soon after and started a forty-year career as a midwife, dentist, storekeeper and sage. Totch was typical of most men that lived off the land and sea. His jobs were fisherman, alligator-poacher, raccoon trapper, and crabber. He served in the 87th Infantry during the second world war and most notably fought in the Battle of the Bulge. Totch was decorated for his bravery with a Bronze Star. He had rescued his platoon from heavy machine-gun fire by crawling forward (no doubt like an Everglades Loggerhead Turtle) to throw a grenade into the German encampment. In addition to the Bronze Star, Totch was awarded a Purple Heart, three battle stars, European and African Theatre Campaign ribbons, a sharpshooter's badge and a Good Conduct Medal. He knew that his upbringing in the Everglades taught him skills which were ideal for what he had to endure in warfare. His superiors recognised this immediately which is why he needed so little training and preparation prior to being shipped to England and then onto the borders of France, Luxembourg and Belgium.

During the 1940s and 1950s, Barron Colliers Rod and Gun Club became a hideaway for a different sort American citizen. The rich and famous. Apart from the celebrities, President Eisenhower and other notable people in sport and business would come here for a break from their high-profile lives. Richard Nixon came here in the 1960s and gave the locals their biggest laugh as he fell over the side of his outboard during a sight-seeing and hunting trip. At its peak, the club had thirty-five to forty charter boats busy for most of the year. It was because of this fame that brought Hollywood filmmakers into the city. "Wind Across the Everglades" starring Burl Ives and Christopher Plummer was filmed here in the mid-fifties. Totch landed a role alongside Burl Ives as they wanted someone who looked the part of a Plume-Hunter, could play the guitar and could make up a song or two about the Everglades. This was something Totch had done all his life and he certainly looked the part. He got along with Burl Ives and commented later that Burl had fitted in so well with the locals it would have been hard for an outsider to notice he wasn't one of them. It was later that Totch would declare this period to be the time of his life.

Things changed for Totch in the late 1970s when it was clear he had to stop his way of life which had depended on hard, physical work. Totch had two heart attacks. The doctor told him "No more hard labour, no skinning Alligators and no more commercial fishing!" It would be a normal activity for Totch to capture a 10ft Alligator, haul it into his boat and skin it. He now had huge medical bills and no sustainable income. This was also at the time when the bans on hunting and fishing had brought the local economy almost to a standstill. Tourism was the only decent source of income for locals and the weather and mosquitos made visiting the Everglades unattractive for most people from mid-May to October.

What would Totch do? What would any group of people, or town, do when faced with poverty? Many had increasingly fallen into poverty as the Everglades National Park, together with the despised Federal Government, increased the restrictions on their livelihood. The average income rarely climbed above $17,000. Totch was a natural leader but he inadvertently led the whole town to be arrested. I'm now going to fast forward.

7th July 1983 — Operation Everglades

At 5:30 am on the morning of 7th July 1983, an armed convoy of more than 200 drug agents and police swept into Everglades City. By the end of the day, nearly 50 arrests had been made and more than half of the fishing boats were seized. Over the next two years, the authorities found 350,000 pounds of marijuana and made further arrests of 94 people on Federal charges. In the following five years, more than 300 people in the Ten Thousand Islands area had been arrested and the city was being called one of the most corrupt towns in America. Almost everyone in the area was either a dope smuggler, friends with a dope smuggler or related to a dope smuggler. Almost all the people living in the Ten Thousand Islands, no matter their status or role were implicated or suspected. One suspect, former Justice David McCain of the Florida Supreme Court, was being sought on charges of conspiring to import marijuana.

In news reports, Everglades City's police chief Herman Askron said he was worried about the seizure's effects on the economy of the village of just 600 people, most of whom, he insisted, weren't drug smugglers. With 350,000 pounds of marijuana being seized under the nose of the city's police chief? Really, he didn't know?

United States Attorney Stanley Marcus and Peter F. Gruden of the Drug Enforcement Administration said in a joint statement: "The objective of Operation Everglades has been to identify and penetrate marijuana-smuggling groups operating on the Southwest coast of Florida, particularly Everglades City, Chokoloskee Island and Naples, and ultimately to disrupt the marijuana-smuggling routes from South America and the Caribbean to the U.S."

Demand and Supply

Everglades City had a demand. Demand for something to replace everyday hunting and fishing. Totch was typical of most residents, he needed to replace hard, physical work with another income. Supply was to come from Columbia, South America. Distribution was readily available through high-level dealers in Miami, a straight forward and undetected drive away through marshland, swamps and sawgrass meadows.

In economic terms, it was a perfect match in many different ways. The dealers could see from one glance at a map that the Ten Thousand Islands, with Everglades City at its heart, was more than just a sportsman's paradise. They offered multiple portals for dope smuggling. It offered a poor but skilled community looking for help and that same community had ideal cover and transport to bring marijuana up from South America. Fishing boats and chartered hunting boats were in abundance.

$17,000 a year or $100,000 a night?

Totch had shown himself to be an entrepreneur many times in his life. It was he who, with his uncle "Dollar Bill" had convinced the owner of Joe's Restaurant in Miami to put Stone Crabs on the menu. They called him Stone Crab Joe. The crabs were a big hit and he changed the name of the restaurant to "Joe's Stone Crabs." This is still the most iconic restaurant in Miami and has become an institution. When one of Totch's buddies suggested to him that he should try "pot-hauling," as it was called, now that he couldn't do hard manual work, he was at first reluctant. His reluctance came from a fairly common source. His wife Estelle said at first "If you ever even mention pot-hauling again, I'll have you arrested!"

Although strictly illegal, social attitudes towards marijuana in the 1970s were not as negative as they were about hard drugs such as cocaine or heroin. Totch eventually convinced Estelle that if he made this one run then it would help them survive for quite a while. "But you've got to promise me you'll never go again," Estelle insisted menacingly. He promised.

He started with a friend just using his fishing boat to meet the 'mothership' from South America moored forty to fifty miles off the coast. They would load the boat and bring about 10,000 pounds of marijuana bales ashore on each run. Bringing it through the labyrinth of narrow channels of the Ten Thousand Islands was, for someone like Totch, easy to escape detection. He was like Br'er Rabbit in the briar patch. Going to the mothership could make $100,000. A bale hopper got $25,000 and whoever loaned his van or truck to the smugglers would get $10,000 in cash and he didn't even have to be there personally. This was a serious temptation for a fisherman used to making $17,000 a year with severe restrictions of what, when and where he could earn his living. Totch broke his promise to Estelle without her knowing. He started making his own arrangements after some crooks and dealers in the chain ripped him off; an occupational hazard. He eventually decided to travel to Colombia on his own and meet the producers and chose his own quality bales of marijuana. He flew to Panama, changed planes and arrived in Colombia to meet the 'dope barons' (as they were called then) in mountain villages. This high-risk approach paid off, but was fraught with danger not only from the barons themselves but also negotiating the hazardous terrain of the mountains where the secret growing areas were. For Totch and his supply chain, the paydays became bigger and bigger. He said of those days, "Instead of crawfish, stone crab and mackerel, I loaded my 72-foot shrimp boat in Colombia with all the marijuana she'd float with and drove 'er home across the Caribbean. We thought we'd never get caught and that's why it went on and on." A local shrimp boat captain could make $1.4 million from a single off-load. He would pay a half-dozen men to meet his boat with smaller, faster boats to negotiate the tiny channels leading to the docking areas. Bale hoppers were hired to unload the bales from the small boats to the waiting vans and trucks. How were they ever going to get caught? Ostentation.

The money was too much and too easily come by. From never having anything in their lives to realising they could now have pretty much anything money could buy.

It's a classic story of poor people turning to crime when all else is put out-of-reach and then having no other explanation for their sudden wealth.

From ramshackle abodes to swimming pools

This new local economy worked wonders for the way things looked and felt in the area. Young men who normally wore jeans and work shirts suddenly appeared around town in gleamingly new cowboy boots and heavy, expensive gold chains and watches. Brand new, sleek pickup trucks could be seen driving the roads where old rust-buckets went before. Houses once in desperate need of repair seem to get upgraded in a matter of months. Screened-in porches, air conditioning, paved driveways and even swimming pools became normal. Word got around of the sudden and very conspicuous wealth in Everglades City. Eventually, word got to the Feds.

The Feds strategy

Nab the little guy whose involvement was minimal, put the pressure on until he agrees to testify against the big smugglers and offer a lighter sentence. Alternatively, if they didn't, they'd get a prison sentence for as long as possible; some got 40 years! The Feds knew it took a lot of people to run one of the marijuana boat offloads and if there is someone who starts to tell all then the whole operation becomes shaky. Cracks appeared in the community's resistance. Wave after wave of arrests were made over several years.

The rise and fall of the smuggler's empire

You will have deduced that this is a small town, where everyone knows everyone, where a lot of people are related, where they are proud of their pioneering history stretching over a hundred years, where their hunting and fishing skills and experience were the core of their existence and where crucially that heritage was taken away through despised government interference — as they would see it. Marijuana smuggling had been a way of life for maybe fifteen years and, although illegal, most of the townspeople regarded it as a relatively harmless drug. Hard drugs such as cocaine and heroin were never handled by the Everglade smugglers. Many thought the only people hurt by the smuggling were the Federal Government who were missing out on taxation. Even one of the arresting agents who had been working on Everglades smuggling prosecutions for five years said, "The government took away their living. They're impoverished. Smuggling cannot be condoned but it got to the point where they had to put beans and grits on the table. If one night a good friend tells you he'd give you $15,000 just to borrow your truck, what would you do?"

Eric Weldon, a pastor of the First Baptist Church of Everglades City, was one of the few people to openly denounce the smuggling but was in despair at the corrosive effect that arrests and 'snitching' had done in the area. He was quoted as saying, "The investigations have ruined entire families and at each new arrest, old wounds are opened. Why can't they just get on with it. As long as these people are in jail, this town will suffer."

Another prominent resident reflected the bitterness that had set in." These boys are getting a raw deal. Rapists and killers can get out in three or four years. They're sending our guys up for 40 years. These people were just trying to make a living. I can't condone marijuana smuggling, but I do understand it. I don't know what I would have done if someone asked me to get involved. You never know, lending my truck for a night? I may have done it myself." It is well known that few in the town today regard the smugglers as lawbreakers and the smugglers themselves didn't ever see themselves as criminals.

Strange justice

So what happened to Totch? A man who freely admitted to smuggling but was never convicted. A man who was a war hero but paved the way for an operation that ferried more than 75 tons of marijuana a week from the mountains of Colombia into the 2,000 square miles of the intricate salt-water warren of Ten Thousand Islands. The Feds got him. He was arrested in 1984; ironically, it was for tax evasion. He calmly pleaded guilty to income tax evasion and, though it was a drawn-out struggle, he was granted immunity from prosecution on drug smuggling charges. In 1982, Totch had reported a fishing income of $18,000 but it was claimed he had inadvertently neglected to mention $528,000 in marijuana profits. It took a lot for Totch to become ruffled and he sweetened his deal with the Feds by writing cheques for $1,229,000 and surrendered assets including a shrimp boat, a house, a condominium, apartments and a brand-new Lincoln limousine. He was sentenced to three years on the tax charges, served 18 months but because he refused to name other smugglers got an additional two months for contempt of court. "I would die rather than testify against my friends," Totch said. Unfortunately, his 25-year-old grandson Eddie Rewis was arrested on four pot-smuggling charges but refused to testify against his friends. Totch's grandson got 40 years for his loyalty. He would be due for parole any day now, I think, at the age of 65. Totch passed away in 1996.

To live there or leave?

We have gone back to Everglades City and Chokoloskee many times since 1988, taking our English visitors along to see the wild side (literally) of Florida as well the high spots of the east coast sophistication of Miami and Palm Beach areas. Once when we drove into town, we saw they were having crab racing on Saturday night and the following week they were holding a competition to see who could size stone crab claws the quickest. These days, Ten Thousand Islands is still a very beautiful and natural wilderness but very quiet.

I read this quote in the Miami News a few years ago from a resident. "There are two expressions that no one uses in this town anymore. One is that this town is going to pot. The second is that we are waiting for our ship to come in."

It seemed a brave but poor attempt to soften the view of a very unfortunate period in their history.

As ever,

Paul

PS: At the time of writing, eight states have legalised recreational marijuana use in the United States. They are Alaska, California, Colorado, Maine, Massachusetts, Nevada, Oregon and Washington. Washington DC also allows the recreational use of marijuana. Also, 25 states have legalised medical marijuana.

PPS: In July 2018, Sammy Hamilton, who served 22 years as the mayor of Everglades City, was arrested and faced charges of grand theft and 16 counts of official misconduct. The Florida Department of Law Enforcement (FDLE) and the Collier County Sheriff's Office issued a statement. "Hamilton had exercised autonomous control of Everglades City financial accounts. He has been the sole signature on the City's checks for the past several years, despite the mandates of the city charter that required dual signatures of both the mayor and the city clerk.

The investigation revealed that Hamilton had used his position to steal nearly $48,000 in taxpayer dollars to pay for boat parts, construction materials and equipment and development fees. A different kind of swamp monster.

PPPS: In an echo of the past good times for Everglades City when it attracted sportsman and famous people, Angie and I noticed a framed letter perched on the ticket desk of "Speedy Johnson's Airboat Rides." It was on headed notepaper from the Houses of Parliament, London. John

Major, former Prime Minister of the United Kingdom, had written a very complimentary letter thanking 'Speedy' for the airboat ride through the Everglades. He said how much he appreciated this unique part of America and 'Speedy's' hospitality. As they would say in the Houses of Parliament, "Hear, hear." However, I would say, don't go overboard.

Research material: Thanks to the Washington Post, Naples Daily News, Miami Herald, Miami News and Totch Brown's "A Life in the Everglades."

Everywhere is nowhere. When a person spends all their time in foreign travel, they end by having many acquaintances, but no friends.

Roman Philosopher, Lucius Annaeus Seneca

I have always tried not to fall into this trap. I hope I've succeeded.

Author

One more thing, never give up!

Author

Photographic Permission: Acknowledgements and Thanks

*All Shutterstock: Under Licence SSTK-0B9AA-4693